Lenin, Stalin & Communist Russia

The Myth and Reality of Communism

Studymates

Many other titles in preparation

Lenin, Stalin & Communist Russia

Robert Johnson

www.**studymates**.co.uk

© 2003 by Robert Johnson

ISBN 1 84285 039 3

First published in 2003 by Studymates Limited, PO Box 2 Bishops Lydeard, Somerset TA4 3YE, United Kingdom.

Telephone: (01823) 432002
Fax: (01823) 430097
Website: http://www.studymates.co.uk

Typeset by PDQ Typesetting, Newcastle-under-Lyme
Printed and bound in Great Britain by The Baskerville Press Ltd.

Contents

List of illustrations

Foreword

The century of Russian and Soviet history between 1855 and c.1955 has been characterised as a 'century of suffering'. Yet contained within this period we also have the view that the Revolution of 1917 marked the 'most glorious moment in Russian history'. These interpretations cover the spectrum of historiography of events throughout the Russian Empire and Soviet Union, and form the focus of this Studymate.

We face the conundrum of millions dying from the effects of misguided and inflexible policies, both before and after the events of 1917. Millions dying in the name of ideology. Millions being given opportunities and freedoms previously denied them. And, while the Soviet Union was not the perfect workers' state, it must be borne in mind that foreign intervention made a significant contribution to the unbearable suffering of the people. Only now, with the opening of the Soviet archives, are we able to gain a clearer picture of the great brutalities inflicted upon the peoples of the Soviet Union. Yet, only now can we gain an appreciation of the Soviet perspective.

Robert Johnson's work clearly charts the debates amongst historians regarding the achievements and blatant shortcomings both of Tsarist Russia and the Soviet Union. He provides an invaluable tool for students of this crucial period of history with clear and succinct analyses of the continuing historiographical debates.

Dr Jackie Bennett
October 2003

Author's Preface

Ideologies often damage society. The history of the twentieth century could be seen as the era of totalising ideologies. Convinced of the righteousness and singularity of their cause, ideologues propagated a worldview that was exclusive and determinist. The result of these strongly held and inflexible beliefs was world war and decades of oppression. Only now, as the Soviet Union slips into history and the Third Reich is a distant, nightmarish memory, can this perspective be truly appreciated. The world is now more aware of how dictatorships and extremist ideologies, from fascism to Islamic fundamentalism, can affect not just the citizens of their own states, but the whole population of this globe. Regimes based on extreme ideologies also have a habit of obscuring their true intentions through a smokescreen of propaganda, twisting otherwise benign values to their own ends. Thus Islam is harnessed to serve a war of terror and revenge, or the name of the people is invoked to justify barbaric crimes against humanity.

This Studymate is designed to help you acquire a rapid grasp of the key ideas, events, and arguments that surround the history of communism in Russia, the myths that were invented by the communists to conceal the truth, and the responses of historians to new information now coming out of the former Soviet archives. It is easy to see why so many in the West were beguiled by and enamoured of the idea of communism, but the dark reality of the Soviet Union can only now be fully understood.

Broken into short chapters, each with a summary and a clear list of 'what you will learn', you will find that each section is lucid, easy to digest and packed with useful information. Written in succinct parts, you will also find that you will progress quickly through the book. To help you assimilate what you have read, there are tutorials at the end of each chapter. Historians' opinions are included to show you where arguments have developed and how they have been resolved. These will help you to formulate your own opinions. You will also find a list of recommended reading and useful websites to take your research further. For those new to Russian history, this Studymate will help you to engage in its essentials without wasting time. For those more familiar with the subject, there is still plenty to refresh the memory, and new ideas to explore.

R.A. Johnson

1

Introduction: The Rewriting of Russian History

One-minute summary – Since the opening of the Soviet archives in the 1990s, a new picture of Russian history is emerging. Many of the myths invented by the communists and propagated amongst their own countrymen, or projected into the West, have been exposed as fraudulent. However, this is not the first time that Russian history has been 'revised' in some way. Various schools of thought developed after 1917, many of them deeply affected by ideological standpoints. Moreover, the relative importance of individuals, the people, the wars and the revolutions have been fiercely contested. What seems less in doubt is the way in which communists established a centralised state which was as ruthless in its exercise of power as the old Tsars had been. Sadly for many millions of people who lived, and died, in the Soviet Union, the communists were just as inefficient, unjust and brutal too.

In this chapter you will learn:

▶ an outline of the period
▶ how the Soviets changed history
▶ schools of thought: the liberal perspective
▶ how the West viewed this period of Russian history
▶ how Russian history has changed.

An outline of the period

Russia under the Tsars appeared to be strong, but was weak

Russia had expanded from a small kingdom to a sprawling empire of many nationalities over a period of 500 years. For 300 years, the Romanov dynasty exercised absolute power as rulers, or Tsars, and they passed *Ukase* (edicts) as they saw fit on all matters of state. The people of Russia were not represented in any way and the only other power in the land was the Orthodox Church which supported the regime as a means of preserving stability in society. Yet the nineteenth century was a period of immense change for Russia and its imperial dominions. Industrialisation put pressure on the social structure, as urban workers with no roots in the more conservative countryside challenged low wages and appalling working conditions. An emerging middle class also pursued an agenda of change in the political system, hoping for a greater say in Russia's affairs. Yet these were the minorities, and the greatest mass of the Russian population were peasants in varying degrees of poverty. The neighbour of the developing West, Russia lagged far behind in economic terms and was condescendingly referred to as an Asiatic power, and yet Russia continued to aspire to a 'great power' status purely on account of its size. Russia continued to expand against weaker Asian states, but this process was halted smartly by a war with Japan in 1904–5. Russia was defeated, and the simmering problems of decades of inefficiency and repression erupted in a popular rebellion in 1905.

A century of turbulence followed: war, revolution, civil war, famine and dictatorship

In a weakened state, the Tsarist regime was overwhelmed by a war against Germany and Austria in 1914. All the weaknesses of the system were exposed as transport, supply, industrial organisation, the army and public morale all broke down. In February 1917, Tsarism was overthrown in a popular revolution and a provisional government was established. This government also failed to solve Russia's deep-seated problems and performed equally badly in the war. As faith in the provisional government leadership ebbed away, and before a new elected assembly could convene, a small but growing party of Bolshevik revolutionaries seized power in the capital. Almost immediately this initiated a civil war in which thousands died. To cling on to power, the Bolsheviks tightened their grip over the people, abolished workers' councils and spread propaganda. In the years that followed, ten million people perished in a famine caused by the Bolsheviks' draconian economic policies. Opposition was silenced and the pattern for the future Soviet Union was established: a one-party dictatorship backed by the whip hand of the secret police.

Stalinism cost the Soviet Union a great deal

When Lenin died, Stalin continued to centralise power. He was driven by a desire to 'catch up' with the West but also by a deep fear of opposition, both internal and external. Stalin therefore embarked on an ambitious programme of modernisation, often at the cost of thousands of lives. When opposition seemed imminent, he murdered his rivals, and staged 'show trials' where victims confessed in the hope of saving their families. This process accelerated and soon 'quotas' of those to be killed were drawn up. The aim was to terrorise any opponent into submission. Yet thousands of loyal communists were also murdered or died in the terrible conditions of *gulags* (labour camps). The Great Terror so weakened Russia that, in 1941–42, the Nazi invasion almost succeeded in capturing Moscow in a matter of months. Russians exhibited a stubborn determination in adversity. Despite millions of casualties, including thousands inflicted on their own side by secret police, the Soviet Union gradually pushed the Germans back to Berlin. Stalin still saw the West as a threat, even when Germany had been defeated and occupied in 1945. As a result, the Cold War began: a confrontation between the democratic West and the authoritarianism of the Soviet Union. Stalin was the architect of the distrust between the two sides and he never ceased to exercise his influence. Fortunately he died before he could initiate another round of mass killings in his own country.

How the Soviets changed history

The Marxist interpretation of the past had a modern political agenda

When the communists came to power in Russia in 1917, they 're-wrote' history to suit their doctrines. The motive was political: they wanted to re-educate everyone to believe in the benefits of communism and, if this involved manufacturing history, or being economical with the truth, then so be it. Soviet Russia was not an open society and only a small elite had access to the archives of the Communist Party. As a result, those documents which showed the party had made mistakes or committed atrocities were concealed. The version of events which the Soviet Union wanted people to hear was the only one permitted. Historical symposia in the Soviet Union were little more than political rallies, and any deviation from the official line could land individuals in trouble. Since party membership was a necessary prerequisite of any career or advancement, the majority were unwilling to risk everything by opposing the regime. The Cold War made this discipline even more heightened, and few would want to be labelled an 'enemy of the people'.

Lenin was a celebrated figure in Soviet histories

Marxist historians were therefore under pressure to interpret the events before and after the revolution in the narrow criteria of ideology. Lenin instructed, for the purposes of modern political propaganda, that the emphasis should be placed on the heroic role of the proletariat (urban workers) and the 'inevitability' of their victory in 1917. All other groups were diminished in importance in the works of M. Pankratova, Aaron Avrekh and A.B. Shapkarin. Soviet history also placed a considerable emphasis on the instrumental role of Lenin as a popular leader of the people. The proletariat had reached a stage of 'class consciousness' that made them ripe for revolutionary action in 1917 (and they had formed Soviets, or councils), but it was Lenin who pointed them in the right direction and inspired them with his famous slogan of 'All Power to the Soviets!'. Of all the revolutionaries, he alone understood the aspirations of the working class, it was said. They emphasised his humble birth, his arduous exile, his great intellectual ability and the way in which he achieved the deliverance of the Russian people from the 'slavery' of capitalism. They saw him as the architect of modern Russia, a positive pioneer and a genius. So highly regarded was he that when he died they embalmed his body and laid it under a glass case in a specially built mausoleum in Red Square, Moscow. Millions shuffled past his body every year until 1989. The irony of all this was that Lenin left behind a regime more powerful and dictatorial than Tsarism and, after his death, he was converted into a quasi-religious icon just as the Tsars had been.

Communism produced a form of 'politically correct' vocabulary

Stalin used and developed the idea that Lenin had been 'infallible' in order to further his own aims. It became a dangerous blasphemy to criticise anything that

Lenin had done and, before long, it was Stalin who was the mouthpiece of Lenin's will, even if what Stalin said bore no resemblance to Lenin's intentions at all. Stalinist Russia was full of 'doublespeak', where saying one thing meant quite another. Communist parties in the Eastern Bloc, a region controlled by Russia after 1945, often referred to themselves as 'democratic' even though they were not democratic at all. A form of 'political correctness' sprang up where the words 'revolution' or 'proletariat' became a sort of passport to acceptance. At all meetings, for example, speakers would invoke the word 'proletariat' to legitimise what they were saying.

How the West viewed this period of Russian history

This period of Russian history is significant because it influenced the twentieth century profoundly. After the struggle against fascism in the 1940s, the Soviet Union's vast military might and its ideological message (that was simple and appealing to many in the non-Western world) was the greatest threat to the West's security. The secretive nature of the Soviet Union, and the communist commitment to overthrowing the capitalist economies, naturally made historians of the West cautious if not hostile. Even though the Soviet Union had been an ally of the West in the Second World War, the Cold War made criticism of Russia more likely. However, there were many left-wingers in the West who *wanted* to believe that communism was a viable alternative to the inequalities of wealth that seemed to characterise capitalism. The left was more critical of the United States of America than of Russia. Some were even prepared to travel to the Soviet Union and deliberately reported on the success of the Soviet experiment even when the inefficiency and corruption of the system was painfully evident. Views in the West might therefore be categorised as liberal and democratic, or socialist and pro-communist.

Schools of thought

The liberal view was largely concerned where Russia had deviated from a potential path to democracy and the Western model of economic development. Liberal historians were eager to criticise the Soviet view as little more than propaganda. There was a particular dislike of Lenin. He was seen as a figure who had duped the Russian people by his false promises of 'All Power to the Soviets', 'Peace, Bread and Land': he made no concessions of power, he gave Russia years of civil war, he created a famine in 1920–21 and he intended to nationalise the land (that is, take it out of private ownership). The leadership of Russia was the main focus of many studies and naturally so, for the Tsar had been the key decision-maker before the revolution, and Lenin one of the key players after it. The Tsar was regarded as an inept and unfortunate man, but Lenin was an ambitious and ruthless individual. Far from humble origins, he was a middle-class intellectual driven by a desire for revenge when his brother was executed for terrorism. Lenin exploited the unrest in Russia to pursue his own ideological agenda, and in the name of his ideology, thousands were killed or reduced to a form of servitude and fear. The democratic institutions of free speech, freedom of assembly, freedom of conscience and a free press, on which the West was based, were suppressed. Secret police were given a licence to act against any citizen and were only accountable to one party. The emphasis on leadership also tended to mean that liberal studies were focussed on events in St Petersburg and Moscow.

The liberal school of thought had different approaches within it

Within the liberal school of thought, there were many variations and ideas. The 'optimists' view, seen in the work of A. Gerschenkron, was that the fall of the Tsars had not been inevitable and that democracy may have flourished but for the First World War and the exceptional conditions it threw up. Theodore von Laue took a 'pessimists' line, concluding that the forces arraigned against democracy were too great and that a revolution at some time or another had been inevitable. Whatever their variation, liberal historians of the West were generally critical of the brutality and deception of the Bolsheviks, rejecting the 'inevitability' of Soviet victory and the exaggerated views of Lenin. In the final analysis, Lenin seemed to be consumed by a desire for revenge and power and his adherence to the false principles of Marxism brought years of fear and misery to Russia and the wider world.

The libertarians were dissatisfied with the emphasis on leadership

The left-wing historians of the West were unhappy that most studies seemed to be concerned only with the events in St Petersburg or the leaders. They were concerned to retrieve the 'real' revolution that had occurred at grass roots level. Placing the focus on the people, libertarians examined the peasants, the urban workers and events in the provinces of Russia and the old Tsarist Empire. Where liberals pointed out that the October Revolution had been a *coup d'etat* by a minority, libertarians instead suggested that the real revolution had been quietly going on in the countryside from February 1917, as peasants seized land and took reprisals against former landowners. Libertarians were nevertheless unconvinced by the rigid interpretations offered by the Marxists. The danger of seeing everything as being economically determined and the proletarian victory as inevitable was that it tended to deprive the Russians of any freedom of action in history. They were made to appear as bit players in a drama, which obeyed the iron laws of Marxist history. With this approach, the libertarians had a point. At times, even the Bolsheviks did not look as if they were in control of events and the masses had played a key role at certain moments: the February Revolution in Petrograd, the defence of Petrograd against Kornilov, and the Russian Civil War. The chief problem with the libertarian view is that one cannot write the decision-makers completely out of the history of this period. The people were important, but often they were simply reacting to events too, and relatively few took part in the Bolshevik coup in October, which, like it or not, changed the direction of Russian history.

How Russian history has changed

Since the opening of the Soviet archives and the collapse of communism in Russia, the focus has been on re-examining the Soviet era, rather than the period before the revolution. There has been much criticism of the revolutionaries, but equally there has been no attempt to portray the Tsarist system in a more positive light. This is because the openness of Russian society before 1917 made it possible to study the old system, but the Soviet era documents were hidden. The new archives have revealed fresh details which had been deliberately concealed. The opening of the archives, which is still not complete, is a metaphor for events in Russia since the 1980s. The USSR collapsed primarily because the centrally planned economy broke down under its own inefficiency and corruption. To sort out the mess, Mikhail Gorbachev gambled on a new political openness or *glasnost*. Revealing problems honestly and openly was supposed to make the Soviet Union more efficient through restructuring or *perestroika*. In fact, the system could not cope. There were demonstrations, unprecedented criticisms in all the media and an unwillingness to co-operate any longer. The mood was sensed in the Eastern Bloc too and the Berlin Wall was torn down by the crowds. The Soviet Union began to crack up as each of the national minorities asserted their independence. In the case of the archives then, the openness of the sources has exposed the corruption and lies of the Soviet Union. Far from being the great paradise for the workers that communism promised, it was a dreary, inefficient and restrictive place. Foreigners were carefully monitored, the secret police kept up a constant observation and the party ruled all.

The revisionists offer a fresh alternative

The most difficult group to categorise is the revisionist one, for there is barely a consensus within it. Nevertheless, broadly speaking revisionists are those historians who challenge an existing orthodoxy. In the case of Russian history, revisionists take issue with all the other schools of thought. They are critical of the Marxist reliance on rigid theory and propaganda, and equally dissatisfied that Lenin should be condemned as a man incapable of leadership or influence. Revisionists seem to acknowledge the role of the people, but do not wish to exaggerate their role. In many ways, what revisionists are aiming for is a version of Russian history that can be separated from 'agendas' or ideologies. This era of Russian history should be treated dispassionately, using the sources that are now available to reappraise what really happened and why. Revisionists aim to weigh up and assess the most important factors in their relative importance, rather than their ideological significance. Thus Lenin, for example, can be seen neither as the faultless hero of Marxist myth, nor the charlatan adventurer of the liberal view, but as an historically significant individual sometimes influencing events and sometimes reacting to matters thrust upon him. As more material on Lenin is discovered, and new biographies are published (like the one by Robert Service – see Further Reading) a clearer picture of the man is emerging. He was driven by a curious mixture of revenge, deep intellectual convictions and bloody-mindedness. In this sense, he was perhaps closer to Stalin than previously thought.

There is a danger of caricature in Russian history
In some circumstances, it is easy to forget the important comparisons with the West. Russia was autocratic for much of its history, but so were some countries in Europe. When Tsar Alexander II emancipated the serfs of Russia, for example, he did so two years before the United States ended slavery. Tsarist Russia does not look so brutal when one recalls it was only the educated 'troublemakers' who were affected by the *Ochrana* (the secret police). Given Lenin's and Stalin's brutal record later, was it not reassuring to think that both of these men were known to the Tsarist secret police as dangerous individuals? In Britain, the most notorious Irish terrorists were known to the British police force in the same way. Russia's economic backwardness is easily blamed on the Russians, but it was also in part the result of British and French, and later German and American, strangleholds on maritime commerce over continental resources. A lack of capital precluded investment and development at the same rate as the United Kingdom.

Russia was not a failure but achieved much
By the twentieth century, Russia's continental resources, which had been freed up, allowed it to match the West, and enabled the Soviet Union to emerge as one of the three great superpowers of the twentieth century. It was also able to sustain two and a half years of total war against the world's most powerful army, and her allies, on two fronts, between 1914 and 1917, and again in 1941–45, the second time victoriously. The February and October revolutions may appear to have been unfortunate episodes, but these were attempts at real liberation by the people themselves, a liberation caused by the suffering of the war rather than being the fault of the Russians themselves. All the western powers were suffering the same kinds of problems in 1918, and endured hardships just like the Russians in 1941–45.

Tutorial

Progress Questions
1. Why do Western views of Russian history vary so much?
2. What were the 'motors of history' according to Marxist historians?
3. Why were 'libertarians' unhappy with other approaches to Russian history?

Seminar discussion
'The Bolshevik version of Russian history is totally without value today.' Is this true? Try to think about the arguments both for and against the quote. Being able to offer alternatives, and being able to weigh up their merits, will make your work more analytical.

Practical assignment
Create a table of the interpretations in one column and a list of key events in adjacent columns. Complete the cells as you progress through each chapter. This will help you keep track of the historiography as you tackle each part of the history and will produce a handy revision guide at the end of the book.

Study tips
Create a folder of personalities, leaders and their works. Add to this as you work through the book. Organise your notes so that you have a summary of each chapter under clear headings.

2

Russia Under the Tsars

One-minute summary – When Russia began to dismantle the old feudal system of land ownership in 1861, there was wide expectation that the country was moving to a more democratic future. However, this reform was designed to strengthen, not weaken, the autocracy of the Tsars. Since the people had no representation except the regional councils and village communes, frustration led to the emergence of revolutionary organisations. The regime tried to carry out economic reforms, but feared the consequences of industrialisation they could already see in the West, such as the emergence of strong labour movements and socialist ideas. In essence, the Tsars were faced with one insurmountable contradiction. They wanted to retain all the powers and privileges of the medieval autocrats, but they wanted to create a modern, industrialised economy. In the event, the rulers turned to repression and nationalism, and every episode of unrest made them more determined to retain control. The solutions they proposed were 'too little, too late' and a fatalistic resignation began to set in during the years before the war. The Tsar's opponents, however, remained weak and divided. Their tactics were limited to assassinations and terrorism. Even when widespread disturbances broke out in 1905, the revolutionaries seemed to be reacting to, rather than shaping events. Existing economic problems were compounded by the war and it was the misery this brought that led to the popular uprising of February 1917 which overthrew Tsarism.

In this chapter you will learn:

▶ how the Tsarist regime functioned
▶ why there were revolutionary organisations and the state policy of reaction
▶ what economic problems Russia faced and how they were dealt with
▶ the historical controversies that have surrounded this subject.

The Tsarist regime

Russia's scale was both a strength and a weakness

Russia's size, occupying one sixth of the world's land surface, gave the country a 'great power' status. The population, standing at 97.7 million in 1880, provided the manpower for agriculture, industry and armed forces on a massive scale. However, Russia's size was also a disadvantage. Its land frontiers ran for thousands of miles, huge belts of its territory were totally unproductive and its infrastructure was stretched between its dispersed population centres. In the

Crimean War (1854–56), it had proved difficult to reinforce and supply its troops even within its own national borders and Russia was defeated.

The structure of society reflected the Tsar's powerful position
The Tsar was an autocrat with considerable powers. He was able to make laws at will and was the supreme head of state. The Tsar's court consisted of ministers and civil servants, and promotion was often dependent on favouritism. The administrators made up about 3.7% of the population. The clergy of the Orthodox Church, led by the Patriarch in St Petersburg, supported the regime by preaching deference and obedience. The noblemen, the titled aristocracy, had strong links with the army and the church, and they could be relied upon to support the regime. The industrial workers were a small group concentrated in the larger towns and cities, but they were subjected to harsh working conditions and had few rights. The peasants were the largest group in society (83% in the early nineteenth century), who, although freed from a system of serfdom, remained impoverished.

The army and the secret police were the executive arm of the state
The army was a vast and loyal institution, making up 5% of the population. Reforms after the Crimean War by Dimitri Milyutin had improved terms of service, but it was still an organisation that demanded obedience to authority. Much of the Russian army was deployed on internal security duties, and was sometimes used to crush rebellion or break strikes. In addition, the regime was served by the secret police, or *Ochrana*, whose role was to detect and arrest political opponents. In extreme cases, dissidents were executed, but many, like Lenin and his wife, Krupskaya, were simply exiled to the vast empty wilderness of Siberia.

The Edict of Emancipation freed the serfs
The system of serfdom had been abolished by Alexander II by the Edict of Emancipation in 1861. Serfs had been 'tied' to the land to provide service to landowners or to the state. Private landowners could require a serf to work three days a week on his estate (the *Barschina*) or pay a rent (*Obrok*) for exemption. The landlord delegated the day-to-day management of a serf's affairs and the distribution of land to the village commune (the *Mir*), which was dominated by the elderly. Serfs could be bought or sold, their land expropriated, marriages arranged and the law administered over them without representation. The status of a nobleman depended on the number of 'souls' he owned. State serfs had been liable to conscription, but capital punishment was not permitted. The Edict (*Ukase*) of 1861 had been conceived as early as 1855, but Nikolai Milyutin, the 'enlightened bureaucrat' Deputy Minister of the Interior, was cautious, taking several years to consult with the noblemen of the provinces. Twenty-one million serfs were freed along with 20 million 'state peasants'. Peasants received the land they had worked and noblemen were compensated with government bonds. However, the consequences of the abolition of serfdom reverberated throughout

the rest of the nineteenth century.

The Edict had drawbacks and was insincere

The government aimed to recoup its expenditure on bonds by compelling the peasants to pay redemption dues. They had to pay 20–25% of the purchase price and pay for the rest at 6% interest over 49 years. The *Mir* held the land collectively until the payments were complete, which, along with the assumption of the landlord's former responsibilities, greatly empowered the village elders. Alexander was heralded as the 'Tsar Liberator'. Hugh Seton-Watson regarded the Emancipation as more successful, more significant and less violent than the freeing of black slaves in America in the same period. However, the reform may not have been as sincere as it first appears. Debts amongst the nobility had forced them to drive the serfs harder, resulting in an upsurge of violence. The lack of modernisation meant that production was failing to keep pace with the rising population. It was hoped that private ownership would encourage improvements to be made, and surpluses would provide funds for reinvestment and stimulate consumer demand. Nevertheless, Alexander remarked in 1856 that 'it is better to abolish serfdom from above rather than await the time when it will abolish itself from below' suggesting that it was driven by a desire to avoid rebellion and disorder.

The results of Emancipation were not as positive as expected

Many peasants feared change, and were particularly angry that they had to pay the redemption dues for land that they had farmed for years and which they felt they truly owned. Some peasants received less land than they expected, and the average land holding was just nine acres. This would promote intensive farming, but only half of the peasants were able to produce a surplus. Former 'privately owned' serfs received no land and had to serve a further two years after the *Ukase*, but received wages in return. The redemption payments were often high because landowners exaggerated the value of their holdings, but this meant that, in order to pay the dues, the peasants had to return to work for their former masters or rent half their land to the landowner and pay for the rents with crops. Some peasants began to buy up plots from others. The peasants who sold up drifted into the towns looking for work. The terms of the Edict were not always implemented straight away and it was not until 1881 that the transfer of lands was finally made compulsory. The indebtedness of the landowners meant that much of the compensation was absorbed in wiping out debts and little money was invested in agricultural modernisation. Landowners remained in debt so that, by 1905, a third of their land was sold and 50% was mortgaged.

The village communes were empowered

The *Mir* was responsible for the taxation of the whole community and it could control almost every aspect of its agriculture. The effect was to stifle the more entrepreneurial farmers. Peasants could not leave the land until payments for their land had been delivered, and any travel had to be authorised by the *Mir*. The net result of the indebtedness and restrictions of the *Mir* was the continued stagnation of Russian farming. However, it is important to take a balanced viewpoint. New labour was released for industrialisation. The Emancipation passed relatively peacefully (there were 647 riots in the four months after the Edict), and the abolition of serfdom brought a degree of modernisation to Russia.

Alexander also reformed local government in 1864

It followed that with the abolition of serfdom, the political structure, which had relied on a system of deference and ownership, would also need to be updated. The landowners were replaced as the provincial authorities by the *zemstva*. These local councils were responsible for education, health, poor relief, road construction, public services and economic development. Each district *zemstvo*, consisting of 45% noblemen, 40% peasantry and 15% townsfolk and clergy, elected the representatives for the higher level provincial *zemstvo*. In 1870, the towns were able to set up local councils (the *duma*) through elections (males over 25). There was no control over the army or police which were controlled by the central government. Political discussions were also banned and the *zemstva* were restricted in 1865–67 when it was decreed that noblemen should make up 75% of their numbers. However, the *zemstva* provided a useful training ground for those who sought political experience.

Legal reforms also took place in 1864

As noblemen no longer administered justice over their serfs, the legal system was changed. The *zemstva* nominated justices of the peace for three-year terms. The secretive nature of trials was abolished with cases being heard in public. Juries and appeal courts were set up. Lawyers' salaries were raised to prevent bribery. Whilst martial law could still be imposed, Seton-Watson believed the courts were the one place where freedom of speech truly existed. Once again, the legal system provided training for those with political aspirations.

Reforms of the armed forces improved conditions

It was said that before the reforms, families whose sons had been selected for military service would hold a virtual funeral for the departing recruit, so convinced were they that he would never return. The length of military service had already been reduced from 25 to 16 years, but, without any leave, army life was more like a prison sentence. Six-year terms of enlistment were thus introduced, and the use of the army as a place for punishing criminals was abolished. Military colonies (where sons of soldiers were sent as the recruits of the future) were abolished too and conditions in barracks improved. Basic education was made available. In 1874, the introduction of universal military service ended the exemption privileges of the middle and upper classes.

Reforms in education were a step in the process of liberalisation

A.S. Norov, the Minister of Education, abolished most of the repressive measures in Russian education. The number of university students was allowed to increase (1855), lectures on European government (1857) and philosophy (1860) were legalised. Universities were also given greater autonomy. These measures indicated the desire of the government to liberalise education, but the motive was also to produce the sort of educated classes that could emulate the West and replicate its mid-nineteenth century economic success.

The onset of reaction: the Polish revolt was a nationalist struggle

Poland enjoyed a special status in the Russian Empire. In the late eighteenth century, Poland had been a powerful independent nation state, but in the 1790s, Poland had been carved up by Prussia, Austria and Russia. After the Congress of Vienna (1815), the 'great powers' had determined that Poland should remain under Russian rule but be given a degree of autonomy. The Tsar was the King of Poland, and the country had a constitution, a parliament and used its own language in the business of government. A rebellion in 1830 had caused some of the Polish privileges to be eroded, but Alexander II had permitted the restoration of the Catholic archbishopric of Warsaw (1856) and established a new Agricultural Society (1857) to improve farming. The Society became the focus of land reform but also of nationalist aspirations and, in 1861, Alexander dissolved it. In the demonstrations that followed, 200 were killed. The Viceroy, Constantine (the Tsar's brother) was almost assassinated. Concessions were offered in the form of the emancipation of Jews and the opening of a university in Warsaw, but the idea that Poles would be conscripted into the Russian army merely fuelled a full blown revolt in January 1863.

The revolt was crushed but Alexander's policy changed

The rebellion was concentrated in the countryside but not all the landowners sided with the peasant rebels. It was not suppressed until August 1864. As a concession, land reform was carried out and 700,000 peasants were given freehold tenure of their land without any redemption payments. This was a liberal gesture, but Hugh Seton-Watson argued that this was simply a move to divide the Polish peasants from their landowners. Alexander believed the ingratitude of Poland was symptomatic of the rest of Russia and he was disillusioned, but in fact the rebellion was just as much the result of Polish frustration with Russian authoritarian rule. Alexander was persuaded that the only future policy towards foreign minorities should be one of Russification.

Repression returned

It was not just the Polish revolt that changed Alexander's mind about his reforms. An assassination attempt in 1866 by a fanatic called Karakosov also focused his attention on revolutionary opposition. The land reforms had taken years of planning, ostensibly to avoid rebellions, but had they gone too far? Essentially,

Alexander was trying to modernise and yet retain the ancient institutions of power; it was a case of changing to stay the same. Certainly the right wing elites in Russia took exception to Alexander's reforms. This is evident when one considers the steps he took. Censorship of the press was reimposed, and the educational concessions were modified. The government took over the universities again and science was dropped from the syllabus to prevent the spread of atheism. In 1868, the *zemstva* lost their powers of taxation and they were supervised by Tsarist agents. In 1878, a woman called Vera Zasulich tried to murder the Prefect of Police, Trepov, and when she was acquitted it was decreed that she and all other political criminals were to be transferred to a courts martial without a jury.

Revolutionary organisations and reaction

The reforms raised expectations

There was considerable opposition to the regime which Alexander had not expected. In many ways, this was not so much dissatisfaction with the reforms but expectations about the future. The peasants, for example, felt the Emancipation would be the beginning of greater social and economic freedom, but the inadequacy of the reforms and the absence of any further change in their favour caused resentment. The liberal and intellectual groups of Russia expected to see the formation of a *duma*, but the Tsar insisted on maintaining autocracy. The greater freedoms of the early 1860s also encouraged committed opponents of Tsarism to speak out more boldly.

The Narodniki tried to win over the people

A very Russian form of opposition was the Populists movement (*narodniki*) which was formed in 1869 and led by Nikolai Mikhailovsky and Pyotr Lavrov. Their aim was to solve the land issue in favour of the peasants and encourage the village commune as the means to advance to socialism without the need to endure the industrial revolution and its miseries which they could see in the West. They dressed as peasants in a campaign called 'to the people' in 1874, touring the countryside to agitate for reform. Three thousand young activists were met by a disbelieving peasant population. The police, who had been tipped off by the peasants themselves, rounded up 1,600 of the *narodniki*. Undeterred, Mikhail Bakunin, Lavrov and Nikolai Chernyshevsky formed a new group called *Zemlya i Volya* ('Land and Liberty') in 1876, which set out to live amongst the peasants for long periods, getting to know their ways and their beliefs. The first trade unions were also formed by Land and Liberty members in Odessa (1875) and St Petersburg (1878), but the government hunted down the members.

There were a number of opposition thinkers in Russia advocating peaceful change

Russian opposition to Tsarism took two forms in this period. There were those who preferred a gradualist path of change, rejecting, where possible, the travails of the industrialisation of the West, and there were those who wanted violent and abrupt change. The lack of progress in social justice in Russia tended to make revolutionary groups more and more radical. Terrorism had become widespread by 1914. An example of the early intellectual moderation can be found in the work of V. Belinsky, who advocated social literature versus oppression. This was followed by Alexander Herzen, who published the *Kolokol* in exile in London and advocated self-governing communes: it was he who founded populism. But Herzen applauded the reforms of the regime, an idea that did not carry favour with Chernyshevsky whose novel *What Is To Be Done?* (1862) suggested a fundamental change in Russia's social and economic base as the only means for progression. Chernyshevsky disagreed with those who claimed to be his disciples but who advocated violence. D.I. Pisarev called on the people to accept no principle, including Tsarist rule, without question. He wanted to see a radical change in Russia's philosophical outlook, especially its moral and material basis. This prompted the novelist Turgenev to label Pisarev a nihilist: the anarchist flavour of this name appealed to Pisarev.

There were opposition groups prepared to use violence

Until 1869, when the movement collapsed and was exposed, the terrorist cell of Sergei Nechayev was the only example of a ruthless and violent organisation. The murder of one of their own activists brought Nechayev into the open. It was not until 1879, when Land and Liberty split, that a new wave of highly organised terrorism began. Georgi Plekhanov, a Marxist, and P. B. Axelrod formed a group called 'Black Partition' (*Chorny Peredyel*) which continued to advocate change through the peasants. The 'People's Will' (*Narodnaya Volya*) thought that terrorism and violence would act as the trigger for a full scale revolution. They concentrated on assassinations, trying to focus on the Tsar himself. There was an attempt to shoot him (April 1879), then they tried to blow up his train (and got the wrong one) and a bomb was detonated at the Winter Palace in 1880. The other key development on the revolutionary left was initiated by Mikhail Bakunin, a member of the First International (1869) and a Marxist. At this early stage, Marxist ideas were not yet widespread and Bakunin argued with Marx over the methods and philosophy of revolution. He subsequently became an anarchist. All the revolutionaries shared a desire to see fundamental and rapid change (not gradualism) in Russia through the *narod* (people). Yet achieving this amongst a population dedicated to the Tsar seemed remote.

The revolutionaries did not succeed despite the assassination of Alexander II (1881)

Despite the growth of terrorism, Alexander appeared to be moving once again in a liberal direction when he appointed General Mikhail Loris-Melikov (the man who had captured Kars from the Turks and saved national honour in 1878) to solve unrest. Loris-Melikov was appointed Minister of the Interior in August 1880. He released hundreds of political prisoners, commuted the death sentence in many cases and urged the Tsar to consider some power sharing. On 31 March, the Tsar agreed to call a committee that would discuss the reforms. The main proposal was to have the *zemstva* co-operate with the Council of State in deciding on a new constitution. However, before the meeting convened, Alexander was killed the same day when a bomb blew off his legs. Yet the Tsarist regime did not collapse when Alexander was assassinated. Since the revolutionaries offered no realistic alternatives, and enjoyed no mass support, the old system continued.

Tsar Alexander III implemented severe repression

Inevitably after the murder, the new Tsar cracked down on revolutionary groups, but there was a reactionary policy across many aspects of Russian life. This was pre-planned. Alexander III's tutor was Constantine Pobyedonostsev, a reactionary Pan-Slav and senior official in the Russian Orthodox Church. Loris-Melikov was dismissed in favour of Pobyedonostsev. As a member of the Orthodox Church, Pobyedonostsev was convinced that other religious groups and foreign minorities needed to be crushed. Ordinary Russians often resented Jews and Pobyedonostsev encouraged anti-Semitic riots (*pogroms*). In 1891, thousands of Jews were evicted from Moscow and herded into ghettos. This served to fuel nationalistic feelings in some people and thus distract them from discontent with the regime. Minorities became scapegoats. The property of the Catholic Polish church was confiscated (1864) and Warsaw University was closed (1869). Catholics or Poles were banned from government posts, as were the peoples of the Baltic States, the Finns, Ukrainians and Armenians. Finland's liberal constitution was undermined. Estonia and Livonia had their local liberties suspended. A tough policy of Russification was embarked upon amongst the 40 million non-Russians in the empire, including the imposition of the Russian language in all schools. Pobyedonostsev condemned the free press and regarded democracy as 'a fatal error'.

Repressive measures were also imposed in law, local government and education

Pan-Slavism and the desire to re-establish the nobility as the foundation of the regime informed the reactionary policies of Alexander III's government. In July 1889, the position of Justice of the Peace was abolished in favour of a new post: *Zemsky Nachalnik* (Land Commandant). The post holder had to be of noble birth and had jurisdiction over all local government including the *zemstva*. Laws of 1890 and 1892 revised the franchise of the *zemstva*, restricting the popular vote. Certain issues could not be discussed, such as government policy. This was used as an excuse to block and veto almost every proposal of the *zemstva*. R. Charques remarked that this measure 'brought back the breath and being of serf law'. The universities were subject to the revisions of the Minister of Education, I.V. Delyanov. He reduced the autonomy of these institutions (1884) and raised tuition fees (1887). Even in elementary and secondary education, new fees were designed to keep the poorer paid in their place. Parish elementary schools, under the close control of the clergy, were permitted a degree of autonomy. Whilst the educated and wealthy elite continued to produce some of the century's finest cultural works (Chekov, Tolstoy, Tchaikovsky), in 1897 79% of Russia's population remained illiterate.

The accession of Nicholas II did not change the repressive policies

Despite some hope that the death of Alexander III in 1894 (through insomnia and migraines) might bring a new liberal phase in the regime, there was bitter disappointment when Nicholas II continued the old policies. In 1903, Finland's constitution was abolished, in direct contravention of the original agreement of 1815 which had established Russian rule there. Russification was also intensified. Most of the students at the university of Yuriev (formerly Dorpat) at Riga were Russian. Anti-Jewish *pogroms* continued, with 215 outbreaks between 1881 and 1905. At Odessa in 1905, five hundred Jews were murdered. Dmitri Tolstoy, the Minister of the Interior, tried to replace this disorder with a more systematic policy. Jews were forbidden to trade on Christian holy days; they could not settle in the rural areas, they were not allowed to make up any more than 10% of school or university places. Expulsion of 'illegal' settler Jews in Moscow and St Petersburg was encouraged. As a result of this harassment, some Jews formed a Zionist organisation called the Bund (1897), which mutated into revolutionary socialist action in the twentieth century.

Economic problems

Economic reforms were difficult when Russia was poor and its leaders feared change

Although Russia had abundant resources, it lacked capital to develop and exploit them. Russia's infrastructure was especially poor. Worse still, there were many who feared the consequences of industrialisation. The conservative elites believed that it would create disruptive social forces that would destroy the old order in Russia. When Sergei Witte was appointed Minister of Finance and Commerce in 1892, the government's policy changed. Witte was convinced that Russia would only remain a 'great power' if it could take its place amongst the leading industrial nations of the world. He believed the Russian government had to guide that development. What is immediately apparent is the difference here from the development of the countries of Western Europe. In the West, entrepreneurs, private companies and banks drove industrialisation. State intervention was frowned upon as restrictive and free enterprise was the rallying cry of capitalism. Witte was advocating a state-directed industrialisation programme but, unless he was able to generate a spirit of capitalism and enlarge the middle classes, this development would not be easily sustained.

The existing problems

► Serfdom had been abolished but redemption dues kept the peasants in poverty.

▶ This meant there was little chance for the modernisation of agriculture.
▶ Landowners were too far in debt to invest in agriculture.
▶ Industrialisation was small in Russia, but Witte hoped to kick-start it all with railway development (as had occurred in the West?).

Witte's measures were a partial success

Witte knew that Russia lacked the capital to develop itself and the rouble was too weak to compete with other currencies. This was evident when, after low tariffs had caused an influx of foreign goods, Russia raised high protective tariffs in 1891. As a result, foreign loans were brought in, especially from France. Unfortunately, to pay the interest the government increased indirect taxation (thus avoiding the damaging direct income tax of the wealthy) and this burden fell heavily on the peasants. Russia also adopted the gold standard (1897) to give greater prestige to the currency.

The development of the rail network

Some of the foreign capital was spent on the development of the railway network, the most efficient of all transport systems then available. Before 1892, annual railway construction had been limited to 400 miles a year. In the 1890s, that increased to 1,400 miles a year. However, despite this spectacular increase, most of the expansion was in a single line, the Trans-Siberian Railway, which was begun in 1891 and completed in 1902. Given the vast size of Russia, the railway network density was still low compared with other countries (the USA had 257,000 miles but Russia had only 38,750 in 1913). In addition, some lines were still being built for military rather than economic purposes such as the line across Turkestan in Central Asia, although industrial areas were now being linked.

Other parts of Russian industry were developed

Witte urged the development of heavy industries as a catalyst to other economic development, namely iron, steel, cotton, oil, coal and the machine industries. Under Witte's leadership coal production doubled and there were great leaps in other areas, but from such a low starting point, these figures still lagged behind the West. His factory regulations and control of liquor were designed to discipline the work force.

Assessment of Witte's policies: modernisation at a cost

However, most of Witte's policies were not original. Other ministers had sought to stabilise the rouble and encourage in foreign capital. The increase of the national debt, neglect of consumer goods and high taxation of peasants can be regarded as serious disadvantages. Witte benefited from low international interest rates (easier to attract capital and lower national debt). Peasants couldn't improve agriculture and therefore increase productivity – the central problem of Russia therefore remained unsolved. A few peasants made some side earnings from industrial work. The demand for industrial products in Russia itself was low. Moreover, the increase of tariffs raised the price of foreign goods and reduced the purchasing power of the Russian consumers. The price of industrial goods increased still further.

Problems in the Russian economy continued

Peasant farmers found themselves as impoverished at the turn of the century as their forefathers had been. Low bread prices were fixed by the government, but this meant low rates of return for the farmers and particular hardship when the harvests failed as they did in 1891, 1892, 1898 and 1901. Peasant holdings were often small and inefficient and so, when the population of Russia began to rise, the pressure on existing land ownership grew intolerable. The average land tenure in 1877 had been 35 acres, but this fell to 28 acres in 1905. Poverty, 'land hunger', arrears in taxation payments and under-investment continued to plague the agrarian economy. The government's first concern was to strengthen the nobility as the basis of political support for the regime. To alleviate their indebtedness, Land Banks were established in 1886. These were backed by government funds and former state lands that could be purchased by the peasants themselves at favourable rates, sometimes as low as 4%. In addition, new 'virgin lands' were exploited. In 1896, the Resettlement Bureau was established to encourage migration to Siberia. Criminals ceased to be shipped there in 1900 and by that same year some 750,000 peasants had moved. However, the number of peasants in Russia exceeded 97 million in 1895 so the migrations barely kept pace with the natural increase. Peasant land ownership did increase by 26 million hectares in the years 1877–1905, but much land was still privately owned.

There was an increase in production. See below for the figures in millions of tons (from A.J.P. Taylor, *The Struggle for Mastery in Europe, 1848–1918* (1954).)

	Coal	Pig iron	Grain
1880	3.2	0.42	34
1890	5.9	0.89	36
1900	16.1	2.66	56
1910	26.8	2.99	74
1913	35.4	4.12	90
1916	33.8	3.72	64

Yet the poverty in Russia is revealed by the figures for growth of incomes: Britain's between 1894–1913 was 70% whilst Russia's was 50%. Other comparisons like this can be made with the West.

Witte also brought in foreign expertise, and encouraged maximisation of export of food, both of which were deeply unpopular. His financial borrowing made Russia a debtor, especially to France, but Michael Lynch suggests that Witte achieved much by overcoming opposition and inertia. The rouble was based on the gold standard, checking speculation on the currency.

Assessment of Russia's problems
There are two criticisms, that Witte created new problems and worsened existing problems.

Worsening effects
▶ Agriculture suffered in favour of industry.
▶ Peasants remained in poverty (see below) and there was a fall in the standard of living.
▶ The population growth of Russia made the situation worse.
▶ The taxation depressed the home market and led to high prices.

The net effect of all this was to worsen discontent and this led directly to the 1905 Revolution.

New problems added to the effects of modernisation
The size of the urban proletariat increased (to 2.25 million) and they were concentrated in large units (often 1,000 plus). K. Perry in *Modern European History* remarked: 'This size of plant was often an indication of technological back-wardness – labour productivity was low, therefore it was made up of a large labour force'. The conditions for these workers were bad: low wages, long hours, dangerous working conditions, no protections for sickness or unemployment. Strikes and unions were illegal. The number of strikers in 1894 numbered 17,000 but in 1903 it had risen to 87,000. Many of these men were driven by a desire to solve purely economic problems and they were not yet politicised against the regime. The concentrated nature of the proletarian workers, though, did mean that ideas could spread more rapidly. Their workplace discipline made them more conditioned to the discipline needed of revolutionaries. Marxists regarded them as the greatest weapon of communism.

Russian agriculture lacked modernisation
The centre of village decision-making was the *Mir*, and it imposed restrictions on travel and discouraged innovation. Poverty meant that there was little land improvement. Most farming methods were the same as those of medieval times. In 1900, an average acre of Russian land produced 8.8 bushels of wheat, compared with 13.9 in the United States and 35.4 in Great Britain. Although Russia was exporting millions of tonnes of grain each year by 1913, it did so in order to pay for capital investment in industry and at the expense of its people. Witte was dismissed because of the 1905 Revolution in Russia, but his successor, Piotyr Stolypin, continued Witte's industrial policies. Yet Stolypin is also associated with the regime's attempts to create a loyal peasantry. His hard repression during the 1905 disturbances was to be matched by a solution of the agrarian backwardness that was creating discontent.

Stolypin's reforms focused on the peasant majority

Stolypin made it legal for any peasant to withdraw from the commune in 1906 and in 1910 he dissolved all communes that had failed to redistribute land since the Edict of Emancipation. He also introduced civil rights in local administration (1906) and he allocated more state land to the peasants' Land Bank the same year to alleviate the land hunger. Passes for travel between *Mirs* were abolished, individual land ownership allowed the better peasants to grow what they liked or what would produce a profit or surplus for sale, taxation became an individual responsibility not a *Mir* one and land holdings were kept together, not subdivided. Peasants left the communes. According to Kochan this was 50,000 p.a. before 1914 and 2 million p.a. by 1916.

The effects of the reforms were far-reaching but not apparent at first

The old social order was breaking up. Farmers replaced the peasants. What was needed was more time for the reforms to proceed, argued Stolypin. He stated: 'Russia needs twenty years of peace at home and abroad'.

Stolypin failed to solve the agrarian crisis

By 1905, some 20% of the peasantry owned their own land and by 1915 this had risen to 50%. Attempts at consolidation of smaller plots into larger farms were less successful, running at 10% by the outbreak of war. Three million cases were still waiting to be resolved when the war broke out. Lower interest rates at the Land Banks and the migration of more peasants to Siberia were also attempts to solve the problems in agriculture (3.5 million before 1914). However, it was probably a case of 'too little, too late'. The population was increasing faster than the migrations to new land: land hunger was getting worse. Poorer peasants lost out to the industrialisation of agriculture: debts, taxation and higher consumer prices worsened their situation. Agricultural production rose by only 1%. Lionel Kochan argued that a revolution was inevitable unless the agricultural problem could be solved.

The countryside was on the verge of serious unrest

Despite some evidence of success, the intervention of the war brought the countryside to a state of crisis. Even before the war, Stolypin was falling foul of the Tsar and the right wing ministers who surrounded him. He was about to be dismissed when a double agent called Bogrov assassinated him. Mystery has always surrounded the motives of a man who was working for both the Social Revolutionaries' terrorist movement and the state's secret police. Could Stolypin have ever created a loyal mass of conservative land-owning peasants? Historical examples from across Europe refute the idea that land ownership automatically produced loyalty to any regime. In 1905, and again in 1917, some of the most violent disturbances occurred in the countryside.

Historical controversies

The Tsars have received a mixed historiography

W.E. Mosse believed that Alexander II couldn't be regarded as a 'liberator'. He was too cut off from the people, and even the conservatives at court were disillusioned with his reforms. Hugh Seton-Watson also believed that Alexander was trying to reach an unrealistic compromise between a constitutional government and an autocracy. By contrast, P.A. Zaionchkovsky was more optimistic, feeling that democracy could have come in Russia had not Alexander been murdered that day in 1881. Yet the question of Alexander's liberality is to some extent irrelevant: he maintained the system of autocracy and his reforms encouraged the belief that further reform was desirable and necessary. However, to make any of the reforms work, Russia lacked a stable economic foundation. In this period, Russia lagged behind the Western powers despite its huge reservoir of resources. Before the revolution, any writings on the Tsars took the form of sympathetic biographies, and even in recent years there have been attempts to focus on the paternal side of Nicholas II and his relationship with Alexandra, the Tsarina. After 1917, however, Marxist interpretations dominated Russian accounts of this period, stressing the oppressive nature of Tsarism and capitalism, and the grinding poverty they both produced.

Tutorial

Progress questions
1. What were the consequences of Alexander II's reforms?
2. Why were there so many opposition groups in the period before 1914?
3. How successful were the Tsarist regime's economic policies between 1897 and 1914?

Seminar discussion
Was the collapse of Tsarist Russia inevitable? Were the regime's leaders inept?

Practical assignment
Make a complete list of all of Russia's economic problems. Alongside each one, insert a comment on what solutions were attempted and your own assessment of the relative success of these measures.

Study tips
1. Remember that Russia was suffering quite typical problems for central and Eastern European states in this period. Try to judge Russia's position comparatively.

2. Periodically, it is a good idea to review what you have studied. This will help you to train your memory and retain key information. Try to sketch a

summary of the two chapters you have now read. Once you have done this, take a break and then, without looking, try to redraw or rewrite the summary. What have you missed out? Have you missed out what you do not really understand yet? Focus on these difficult areas, or areas you forgot, next time you review in a week's time.

3

Marxism, Leninism and the Early Bolshevik Party

One-minute summary – The Social Democratic Labour Party, to which Lenin and the Bolsheviks originally belonged, has perhaps received an undue emphasis in the history of Russia because of the later success of the communists. It is natural that, in searching for the origins of the force that governed Russia for 70 years, so much is made of the early party, but in 1900, it was an insignificant, small and exiled organisation. Marxists based their hopes for change on urban workers, but these were few in number, dwarfed by the vast rural population. Lenin produced his own hybrid solution to this problem, but none of the Bolsheviks had any practical experience of governing. Nevertheless, the ideas and principles of the party are important: they clarify the ideological basis of Lenin's actions and strongly suggest that he had always possessed an inclination towards centralisation, authoritarianism and brutality against his opponents. On the other hand, these traits may have been forced upon him by circumstance. Whatever his reasons, Lenin always regarded the Russian middle class, the bourgeoisie, as the enemy that needed to be destroyed.

In this chapter you will learn:

▶ the origins of the Social Democratic Labour Party
▶ the ideas of Karl Marx
▶ how Lenin adapted Marxism
▶ Lenin's role in Russian history.

The Social Democratic Labour Party

The Social Democratic Labour Party believed revolution was the solution

There were many discontented groups in Russia before the First World War. Urban workers, the proletariat, endured long hours, low pay and sometimes dangerous working conditions. Overcrowded slum accommodation added to the misery. Yet to these somewhat typical industrial problems were added the inequalities of the political system. The Russian people were deprived of a voice for their grievances. Intellectuals and the middle class were as disgruntled as the seething masses in the cities and the countryside. Only a devotion to the Tsar seemed to keep the country together. The Social Democratic Labour Party, most of whom lived in exile, believed the solution was for Russia to pass through this period of industrialisation, for the workers to develop a sense of class consciousness (an awareness of their misery that bonded them together in class solidarity) and to effect a revolution. Unfortunately, the proletariat in Russia were heavily outnumbered by the peasantry who, it was thought, would always side with the Tsar. Most of the party was prepared to wait until the conditions in Russia matched those outlined by Karl Marx as prerequisites for a successful revolution. Martov hoped to see the peasant enlisted as part of a popular movement that would sweep away the regime, but Vladimir Illyich Lenin disagreed.

Lenin wanted revenge

Lenin came from a comfortable middle-class background and he was well educated. He differed from his brothers and sisters in that he was fiercely competitive and prone to obsession. When his older brother was killed by the Tsarist regime (he was a member of a revolutionary group), Lenin vowed revenge. He dedicated himself to the works of revolutionary literature. Lenin met George Plechanov in 1895, a revolutionary thinker who followed Karl Marx's ideas. Lenin was arrested that same year for revolutionary agitation and exiled in comfortable surroundings in Siberia. Having recently married, he applied for his wife, Nadezhda Krupskaya, to join him and this was permitted. He used the time to develop his ideas, and wrote a pamphlet called *What Is To Be Done?* (1902). He was soon released and spent the next few years in exile outside Russia, briefly returning after the 1905 Revolution. In London, Lenin founded a newspaper, *Iskra* (the spark).

The ideas of Karl Marx influenced many

Karl Marx's ideas were very influential in the late nineteenth and twentieth centuries, promising an inevitable victory for the oppressed urban workers of the world through revolution. In retrospect, after decades of communist rule in Eastern Europe, Russia, Cuba, Cambodia and China, with their brutal secret police forces, denial of human rights, labour camps, and one-party dictatorships, it is hard to see the attraction of Marxism. However, at the turn of the century, Marx's vision seemed to offer hope to intellectuals who were dissatisfied with capitalism, poverty and the autocracies of Europe.

Karl Marx's ideas: Marxism

▶ Marx claimed that his was the first 'scientific' analysis of human society and sociology. In this, he argued his ideas could not be wrong and he stated that his *predictions were inevitable*. To his supporters, this was encouraging and they regarded him as the 'pioneer of socialism'. In fact, he wasn't. There had been plenty of other socialists before Marx (such as J.S. Mill, Saint Simon, Louis Blanc) and his predictions did not, in fact occur. This demonstrates Marx's arrogance.

▶ Marx claimed that all *history was driven by economics*. He called this 'historical materialism'. Whilst this appears to be an attractive way of explaining the 'motor' of history, it ignores the other factors that help explain historical events, such as religious factors in the dissolution of the monasteries, or the English Civil War, or of the military factors in the outcome of the mid-century wars.

▶ Marx believed that all past *history was a struggle between classes*: the exploited and the exploiters. There had been broadly three periods of exploitation. The ancient civilisation had been a struggle between slaves and elites. The feudal society had been a struggle between serfs and the nobles. The capitalist society was a struggle between the bourgeoisie and the proletariat. The machinery of government, *the state*, was the means by which the dominant group maintained its power.

▶ The change between societies was achieved through *revolution*. The oppressed classes developed a *'class consciousness'* (that is, a knowledge of their oppressed situation and a realisation that, by collective revolutionary action, they could overthrow their oppressors). Revolutions would be bloody but were the only means by which a society could be changed.

▶ When the proletarian revolution occurred, Marx believed there would need to be a brief period called the *Dictatorship of the Proletariat*. During this time, class distinctions would be eradicated (if necessary, by force) and a classless society would be enforced (money, private property, ranks, authority would be abolished too). Eventually there would be no need of a state and it would 'wither away'. In reality all communist regimes strengthened the state to continue to rule.

Interpretations of Marx have been critical

▶ When Marx drew up the Communist Manifesto, he emphasised the inevitability of success because it was a call to arms for the German working class. His ideas have since been criticised for being *too determinist*.

▶ All too often after revolutions, *a dictatorship* of one man or one party has come to power to 'restore order' and they all claim to exercise power in the name of the people.

▶ He predicted the English working class would be the first to revolt because England had the most advanced industrialised society. When it didn't, he *blamed religion* (the 'opium of the masses'), but it had more to do with the English character that favoured moderation, the existing democratic system, constitutional monarchy and universal suffrage (1884), the prosperity of Britain, the well-established system of equality before the law, and nationalism. Marx completely *underrated nationalism* as a sentiment that bound the classes together.

▶ Marx had *no interest in the peasantry* of Europe and underestimated their importance in social unrest. He condemned them all, thinking they were fit only to serve the old feudal system. He hated their conservativism, religious devotion and patriotism.

Lenin's adaptation of Marxism: Marxist-Leninism

Lenin wanted 'two revolutions in one' led by a Red Guard
Plechanov had identified that Russia's problem was that:

▶ The proletariat were small in number and uninterested in politics.

▶ The country was still in a feudal stage and a bourgeois revolution would need to occur before a proletarian one.

▶ Capitalism was still underdeveloped.

▶ The revolutionaries were still essentially only the intellectuals.

Lenin argued that the bourgeoisie in Russia, although small, would try to overthrow the Tsar just as other middle-class movements had done in the West. At that moment, he believed the proletariat must immediately make their own bid for power, whilst there was still confusion. However, to prevent the forces of order uniting against the workers, Lenin advocated the formation of a Red Guard, a professional force of revolutionaries who could lead and organise the proletariat. Following Marx's lead, Lenin argued with Martov that the peasantry could have no role in a revolution. He favoured a highly disciplined (and more easily controlled) group of conspirators, ruthless and not moved by pity. Given the underdeveloped nature of working-class political consciousness (in other words, they did not support the Bolsheviks), Lenin felt it was necessary to 'lead' them with his revolutionary elite.

The Social Democratic Labour Party split in 1903
Disagreements in the Social Democratic Labor Party led to a split in 1903 (formalised in 1912). Lenin's smaller faction was ironically called the Bolsheviks (the 'majority men') and Martov's larger group was called the Mensheviks (the 'minority'). This situation had arisen because of a party meeting. Lenin's faction had lost in a vote (28 to 22) about a resolution on the role of the peasantry in the party. The Mensheviks eventually all left the meeting, feeling the matter was closed, but Lenin and his friends continued to argue. Eventually, when many of the Mensheviks had gone and Lenin was sure he would win a re-vote, he proposed the same resolution, styling his supporters, the 'majority' men. This titling of his group reveals the importance of propaganda to Lenin. What the Bolsheviks claimed to be and what they actually were was quite different. They became

masters of 'doublespeak' (saying one thing but meaning quite another). Both sides, Mensheviks and Bolsheviks, tended to reject acts of terrorism in favour of concerted propaganda campaigns, although they spent most of their time in exile arguing with each other. Moreover, many historians now agree that it was Lenin's abrasive and uncompromising manner that caused the party split in 1903.

The Social Revolutionaries were the most significant group of the period

Although the Marxists under Lenin were eventually successful, it is easy to forget that, before the war, the most important resistance group in Russia were the Social Revolutionaries or SRs (formed in 1901). They inherited the Populist tradition, being made up of students who saw Russia's future in the solution of the land question. They advocated the nationalisation of the land, but focused on terrorist activity and helped agitate unrest in rural areas in 1902. Lionel Kochan has pointed out the ambiguity of some of their ideas, for there were some who favoured the urban workers as a revolutionary force. Thus the official party programme envisaged a peasant rebellion spearheaded by the urban proletariat. It was the growth of terrorism, though, that caused the Minister of the Interior, Phleve, to remark in 1903: 'What this country needs is a short, victorious war to stem the tide of revolution'. Tsar Nicholas II certainly feared the SRs because of their terrorist assassinations.

The SRs were the most popular opposition group

On the more moderate wing of the SRs were the *Trudoviki*, a group that represented peasants' interests in the *Duma* assemblies of 1906 (see Chapter 4) and amongst them was Alexander Kerensky, who rose to prominence in 1917. Nevertheless, in the early 1900s the leading spokesman of the SRs was Victor Chernov. He hoped that peasants would be able to avoid having to be 'proletarianised' in cities and could move straight to a form of socialism based on the peasant commune (the *Mir*). By 1905, about half of the SRs' supporters were peasants who had recently migrated to towns and cities, and who were finding the conditions tough. Crucially most of them had maintained their links with families still in the countryside. This made the SRs a truly representative organisation. Later, in late 1917, the SRs won the national elections, but the Bolsheviks moved against them, precipitating a gruelling civil war.

Lenin's role in Russian history

How important was Lenin in changing Russian history?

Lenin has been so celebrated and vilified as an historical figure, that it is difficult to separate the image of Lenin from the real man underneath. Robert Service has done the historical world a great favour recently in publishing an honest and accurate account of Lenin based on the archives now available, but previously denied to others. What emerges is that Lenin was an apparently ordinary man driven by a passion so consuming that it led him into quite exceptional brutality. The inspiration for that personal drive was multi-faceted, but was primarily his reading of Karl Marx. Marx offered a radical solution to the inequalities that had been thrown up by the industrial revolution in Europe. Lenin translated Marx's theory into action. He was always demanding that something be *done*. In the revolutionary turmoil of 1917, he was to be given his chance. However, we should not assume that, just because Lenin got into power and set up the apparatus of the Soviet Union, that his rise was inevitable. On several occasions, Lenin was defeated and one could argue that, but for the war, Lenin would have remained in exile and obscurity. Equally the forces that acted upon events were often more important than Lenin. Revisionist historians tend to believe that Lenin was important at certain junctures in Russian history, but that he was irrelevant at others. For example, to write a history of the October Revolution without acknowledging Lenin's decision-making would be a mistake, but elevating him to the status of key decision-maker throughout 1917, as Soviet historians tended to do, is a gross exaggeration.

Can individuals change history?

Lenin's role in history raises a more general, but more significant question about the role of the individual in history. Do we make our own destiny, or are we driven by events and circumstances around us? There are many examples throughout history of exceptional individuals who start with little and yet emerge as influential people, such as inventors, statesmen and soldiers. The study of their characteristics often reveals a powerful personal drive that enabled them to inspire others around them or to persevere when setbacks would have limited others. Biographers of Lenin have identified these character traits in him. Yet what appears to be the result of a gifted person may have been the coincidence of many other factors: being in the right place at the right time, luck, or a deliberate myth-making exercise that made them seem more important than they really were. All these are true of Lenin's career too. The most accurate judgement might be that what happens to individuals is a *combination* of 'circumstance' and 'personal effort'. We do not entirely dictate our own futures, but we do have the power to influence and shape the outcomes of our lives. This means that Lenin was perhaps able to exploit a situation that he found himself in. Whilst Lenin achieved political power in Russia and tried to establish communism, he never achieved his real ambition of bringing about a world revolution.

Trotsky was a leading historical figure in Russian history

Lev Bronstein, Trotsky, was the son of a rich Jewish farmer who was arrested for inciting strikes and, like Lenin, exiled to Siberia. He married in prison and escaped to Paris where he met and lived with a Russian art student, Nadia Sedova. In London, Trotsky joined Lenin but refused to accept Lenin's arguments in 1903 and became a Menshevik. Trotsky's concern was that Lenin's concept of a revolutionary elite would lead to dictatorship. In 1905 he added to his skill of writing by developing a flair for oratory and in 1917 he was to inspire thousands with his speeches. Shortly after his return to Russia that year, he joined the Bolsheviks and demonstrated his powers of organisation by orchestrating the October Revolution and directing the Red Army during the Civil War. When Lenin died, Trotsky continued to warn that Russia could slide into dictatorship so Stalin, who was aiming for absolute power, isolated him, then exiled him. When Trotsky continued to speak out against dictatorship, Stalin's agents tracked him down in Mexico and murdered him with an ice axe in 1940.

Trotsky's legacy was long-lasting but perhaps misleading

Trotsky became the darling of left-wing intellectuals in the West because he had always advocated an idealised form of communism and world revolution at a time when Russia appeared to have become a brutal dictatorship. Students proudly claimed to be Trotskyites. However, the real Trotsky was not quite so romantic and he ordered brutal reprisals against all 'class enemies' during the Civil War. His demagoguery on the speaker's platform has a resonance with Hitler and he was clearly ambitious; even Lenin warned that Trotsky was a threat to the revolution. He was disliked by many other Bolsheviks.

Stalin profoundly influenced Russian history

Stalin inherited a position of great authority in communist Russia and he manipulated his authority to dispose of rivals. He then used his absolute power to tighten the discipline of the Soviet Union and to drive forward industrialisation. The command economy he established and the power of the centralised state in the hands of a few were the legacies he bequeathed to the Soviet Union after his death. But there was also the cost in lives. D. Volkogonov wrote: 'Whether the thousands of buildings in the 'Stalinist' style of architecture, the canals, the highways, blast furnaces, mines and factories – built to a large extent by the slave labour of millions of anonymous inmates of the *gulag* – or nuclear weapons, his traces are steeped in blood'. During his reign of tyranny, Stalin never ceased to invoke the memory of Lenin and his achievement. Leninism became a state religion with huge paintings of him draped from buildings, alongside slogans of the revolution. All these were designed to inspire the masses with loyalty and action. Failure to express your support for Lenin and Stalin became an offence that could lead to prison camp sentences or death. The Soviet citizens learned to live with this in a Janus-faced world. The slogans were chanted, and not one spoke out against it, but it all seemed increasingly false. The Russians oscillated between their characteristic bonhomie and sense of fun, and their philosophical resignation to the monotony of reality.

Tutorial

Progress questions
1. Why did both Marx and Lenin believe their predictions were inevitable?
2. What caused the Social Democratic Labour Party to split in 1903?
3. Why was the Social Democratic Labour Party so ineffective before 1917?

Seminar discussion
'Violence was as fundamental to Marx and Lenin as it was necessary.' Is this true? What does this mean for modern protestors?

Practical assignment
Write an essay of about 1,000 words in response to the following question: 'Lenin's ideas were a perversion of Marxism and of the situation that Russia faced; they could only lead to further misery and bloodshed'. Assess the validity of this statement.

Study tips
Try to get a firm grasp of Marxist theory. You will be expected to know how it works in order to understand why Lenin made certain decisions later. It is a useful way to understand the thinking of the Soviet Union during the Cold War too.

4

The Crucible of Russia's Problems, 1905–1917

One-minute summary – There is a sense that the Tsarist regime was fighting a losing battle in the first decade of the twentieth century. Against a background of rapid economic change and a social transformation to a modern industrialised society, and faced with a growing chorus of opinion that demanded power sharing, the Tsar and his ministers resembled King Canute trying to hold back the tide. The most striking evidence of Russia's underlying problems was the outbreak of the 1905 Revolution. Military defeat often brought political and social upheaval in Europe: France and Austria experienced this in the nineteenth century, in 1870 and 1867 respectively. Disasters in war were certainly the catalysts for revolutionary action in Russia in both 1905 and 1917. This means that foreign policy must also be examined when trying to locate the causes of these revolutionary outbursts. However, the nature of the uprisings in 1905 was very different from that in 1917, and clear distinctions should be made in their significance. What is certain is that Russia's deep-seated problems (and consequently the grievances of the people) were at a tolerable level for years, with discontent simmering beneath the surface. When a crisis occurred this discontent burst onto the streets and lanes. Whether the regime could ever have averted these crises is a matter of debate.

In this chapter you will learn:

▶ the significance of the 1905 Revolution
▶ why the 1905 Revolution failed
▶ what Lenin learned from the 1905 Revolution
▶ the 1905 Revolution and historiography
▶ how Russia's foreign policy led to war
▶ how Russia responded to the First World War.

The 1905 Revolution

The 1905 Revolution illustrated the extent of Russia's problems

The Revolution of 1905 was sparked by the humiliating defeat of Russia in the Russo-Japanese War (1904–5), but it was also the culmination of years of unrest. In 1902, there had been a series of peasant riots, followed by a string of industrial disputes and student demonstrations. The Chief of Police in Moscow had experimented in the control of this unrest by the introduction of 'police socialism' in 1902. It attempted to meet demands for improvements in hours and wages in order to avoid more violent outrages. The most successful organisation that was set up under this scheme was the Assembly of Russian Factory Workers, which attracted 8,000 workers in just one year. It was led by Father Gapon and the demands they drew up included economic and political measures: an eight hour day, reduction of indirect taxation, an end to the war, a political assembly, equality before the law, and political freedoms.

The Bloody Sunday massacre was a turning point
When Gapon accompanied a march to the Winter Palace in St Petersburg on 22 January 1905, the crowd swelled to 150,000. The advance of this multitude panicked the armed police cordon and they opened fire. There are estimates that as many as 1,000 were killed and wounded. More than any other incident, 'Bloody Sunday' undermined the authority of Tsarism in the eyes of ordinary people. A strike wave followed, with 2.7 million workers protesting by 1906. The strike of the railway workers was arguably the most damaging, with cities brought to the verge of starvation.

Unrest spread to the peasants and the armed forces
In February 1905, the first serious peasant unrest began in the Kursk region, but this quickly spread to the rest of European Russia. The All-Russian Peasant Union articulated their demands, but this was little more than a front organisation for the SRs since its demands were identical to the terror groups'. Most of the rioting involved local revenge on landowners and property. Troops were deployed to the 3,228 most serious incidents. Yet the position of the armed forces was crucial in the disturbances. With some of the best units away in the Far East fighting Japan, some units mutinied and navy crews at Kronstadt refused to co-operate. The most famous mutiny was that of the battleship *Potemkin* (June 1905), where the men killed some of their officers and shelled Odessa before giving themselves up in Romania. In September there was a general strike of workers in St Petersburg and barricades appeared in many of the major cities of Russia.

The government's initial reaction was panic
At first there was panic. Witte was dismissed, then recalled. He negotiated a settlement with Japan and urged political concessions at home. The regime curbed the military disturbances by using non-Russian troops to put down Russian rioters and vice versa. Promises of better pay and conditions also won over many soldiers and sailors.

Did the defeat cause the revolution?
The existing problems that Russia was suffering were the cause of the revolution, but the defeat certainly acted as a catalyst. With thousands of troops in the Far East, and the regime appearing to weaken, there was widespread unrest. Much of this may have been opportunism, or just anger, not really directed against the regime itself. Certainly, the regime was shocked by the violence and bloodshed

Long-term causes

Workers: ▶ angry about long hours, low pay and bad working conditions	Peasants: ▶ wanted land ▶ angry about poverty and high taxation
Intellectuals and middle classes: ▶ No national assembly to exercise power ▶ Controls in universities resented	National minorities: ▶ Wanted autonomy or independence ▶ Angry at policy of Russification

Government responses

▶ Tsar in absolute power. Concessions feared lest they lead to revolution.

▶ No free press, no freedom of speech, political parties banned.

▶ Secret police.

▶ No rights for foreign minorities.

▶ High taxation to fund Witte's industrialisation drive.

Short-term problems

No solution to economic slump in 1902 which led to increasing unemployment.
Poor harvests in 1900 and 1902; hunger in the countryside led to unrest.
Defeats in the Russo-Japanese War: leaders appeared weak, national humiliation.
War shortages of food and fuel: prices increased.
22 January 1905 'Bloody Sunday' – peaceful demonstration fired on. Resulted in a wave of strikes, violence by peasants, riots in cities and widespread demonstrations.

Figure 1. Causes of the 1905 Revolution.

amongst the peasantry in the countryside, previously regarded as the loyal bulwark of Tsarism. This generated a great deal of pessimism for the future.

The *Dumas* offered a chance for democracy in Russia

Some liberal thinkers formed themselves into the Constitutional Democratic Party ('Kadets') in October 1905, and they demanded an elected assembly based on universal suffrage. On the left, revolutionary groups were taken by surprise by the events of 1905. In St Petersburg, for example, no revolutionaries played any part in the spontaneous emergence of the first *Soviet* (Council) made up of 500 men from 96 separate trade unions. Nevertheless, Leon Trotsky (real name, Lev Bronstein) soon captured the imagination of many workers with his skilful oratory, and the Soviet became Menshevik in outlook. In November, the Soviet tried to co-ordinate a second general strike (the first was in October), but it failed. The Tsar took the sting out of the political demands by promising a *Duma* (assembly) in the October Manifesto. It also offered freedom of speech, of assembly, of conscience and liberty for the individual. Those liberals who accepted the terms were known as Octoberists, but some expected further concessions from the Tsar. However, in November, the Tsar cancelled peasant redemption payments and called on them to return to peace and order.

The concessions of 1905 were a sham

When the army began to restore order and troops started to return from the Far East, the Tsar acted against the revolutionaries. The leaders of the Union of Peasants and the St Petersburg soviet were arrested. In December, an insurrection in Moscow, in which some Bolsheviks played a minor part, was destroyed with the loss of 1,000 lives. Far-right groups, such as the Union of the Russian People and terror gangs called the 'Black Hundreds' lynched reformers and stirred up anti-Semitic propaganda. This set a precedent. The more the revolutionaries fought back with terrorism and assassination (2,999 died in these murders), the more the new premier, Stolypin, responded with counter-terror. Field Courts Martial were established and 1,144 people were executed. Newspapers and unions were closed down. Worse still, the Tsar passed the Fundamental Laws just before the opening of the first *Duma* in May 1906. The Tsar retained his autocratic powers, including control of foreign policy, the executive, and the armed forces. An upper house, the Council of the Empire, would give its consent to any bills offered by the *Duma*, but the Tsar selected half its members. The Tsar could appoint and dissolve the *Duma*, and rule by decree when it was not in session.

The *Dumas* failed but were significant in their very existence

The first *Duma* was dominated by the Kadets, but their demands that the upper house be made responsible to the *Duma*, and that crown lands should be given to the peasants, merely compelled the Tsar to dissolve the whole assembly. When some of the Kadets went to Finland and urged people not to pay taxes until their demands were met (the Vyburg Manifesto), they were denied the right to reelection. The government tried to interfere with the elections of the second *Duma* but about a quarter of the delegates were radicals, including 54 Social Revolutionaries and 34 Social Democratic Party men. The second *Duma* lasted three months. A new electoral law restricted the franchise and the third *Duma* was more conservative, being made up mainly of landowners and industrialists. The *Duma* lasted until 1913 and was replaced by a fourth. These conservative *Dumas* co-operated with Stolypin. The most important reform they managed was a welfare measure that introduced accident and health insurance in 1912. The Land Commandants were also replaced with Justices of the Peace, and, in conjunction with the local *zemstva*, there were improvements in elementary education. By 1914, half of Russian children were getting an education (7.2 million). Indeed, Hugh Seton-Watson believed that the *Dumas* represented a truly democratic advance when, before 1905, the existence of an assembly whose dealings were published in the press was unthinkable.

What is a 'revolution'? Was the Revolution of 1905 a dress rehearsal for 1917?
It is difficult to argue that the 1905 Revolution was some sort of preparation for 1917. In many ways it was more of a rebellion than a revolution, a spontaneous expression of anger at the conditions, rather than an attempt to overthrow the Tsar. A revolution is normally defined as a change in leadership, a violent or abrupt change, or perhaps even an attempt to overthrow a ruler. Serious rioting, if political in nature, might be described as 'revolutionary' unrest. In the case of the events of 1905, it is difficult to consider it a revolution, except that there had been widespread unrest involving thousands of people, and that a *Duma* was created, thus altering the political arrangements of the country. However, in reality, power still rested with the Tsar and the uprisings were all crushed. Trotsky remarked that, but for a few broken bones, the Tsarist regime was strong and well. Whilst 'the masses' had been involved in violence, the numbers who wanted to see the end of Tsarism were a minority and even the *Duma* officials had been opportunists using the disturbances for their own interests. Nevertheless, the anger people felt was genuine enough.

Why did the revolution fail?

▶ Opposition to the Tsar was divided. The traditional left-wing view was that the liberals were pleased by the concessions that stopped short of involving the masses in government. With this bourgeois leadership gone the opposition began to break up. The Bolsheviks, like Trotsky and Lenin, felt the middle classes were the main reason why the revolution had failed. That the middle classes were also their ideological enemies was no mere coincidence. However, this gives the impression the working classes were incapable of independent action (not true of 1905 or 1917) or that the working classes were pursuing a political agenda.

- ▶ The Tsar's will to resist was another reason for the failure of the 1905 Revolution. His initial panic was replaced by a determination to retain power. In 1917, this will left him and the elites abandoned him.

- ▶ The Tsar possessed the means to resist. The army remained loyal despite the defeats in the Russo-Japanese War. The generals were also loyal. This was not the case in 1917.

- ▶ Witte gave useful advice but he resigned after the revolution had been contained.

- ▶ The opposition lacked the will to overthrow the regime. The political elite regarded the Tsar as the rightful authority, as did most peasants. Few wanted to see the Tsar removed, another contrast to 1917. The opposition also lacked its own military force to do anything about the Tsar's troops.

Few of the leaders benefited from the Revolution
- ▶ Phleve: assassinated in 1904.

- ▶ Witte: Prime Minister of the *Duma* but resigned in 1906.

- ▶ Gapon: His march had been pro-Tsar and it had been set up by the police with Trade Union backing. Gapon was murdered by SRs who were convinced he was a traitor.

- ▶ The *Duma*: Due to meet for the first time in May 1906, prior to its opening, the Tsar passed the Fundamental Laws which retained for the Tsar the right to veto any legislation. The Social democrats called for a strike but the army had crushed the opposition and Nicholas felt strong enough to make a stand. The Laws undermined the *Duma* as soon as it met.

What Lenin learned from the 1905 Revolution

Lenin was surprised by the peasant involvement in 1905 and it appeared he began to consider whether the peasants could play a role in the revolution. His ideological sensibilities did not permit him to consider them important, but he suggested that, under proletarian leadership, there might be a role for the masses. However, it was essential to train a revolutionary elite of professionals and propagate the Marxist-Leninist doctrine throughout the Russian Empire. New efforts were made to smuggle newspapers and pamphlets into the country. One of the operatives was Josef Stalin. Trotsky, like Lenin, firmly believed the middle classes had been to blame for the failure of the Bolshevik rising in Moscow. This was ironic since both Lenin and Trotsky were middle-class intellectuals. What neither admitted was that the revolutionaries had played little part in the events of 1905, and he been late or reactive to other events: a far cry from Lenin's desire to shape the course of the revolution with a Red Guard.

The 1905 Revolution and historiography

The Marxist interpretation emphasised the role of the proletariat and bourgeoisie

The Soviet view of the 1905 Revolution was to celebrate the rising of the proletariat in Moscow. This event was used as evidence that the workers had reached a level of class-consciousness that made them ripe for revolution. Their failure was portrayed in heroic terms, caused by the oppressive and overwhelming force of the Tsarist regime. Trotsky argued that the revolution could have succeeded but the middle classes sided with the regime against the workers because they grew frightened of the mob. There is a grain of truth in Trotsky's remarks, but the rioting terrified many people, not just those with property. His remarks were also directed against the *Dumas*. The progressive weakening of the working class membership after the first *Duma* of 1906 appeared to be the result of deliberate collaboration by the middle classes, but in fact it was the Tsar who was altering the franchise, and the Tsar was unwilling to share power with *any* class.

The liberal view examined the leaders

The emphasis of the Western interpretation was on the leaders and the events in St Petersburg and Moscow. This focused attention on the decision-makers, like Nicholas II, or influential individuals like Father Gapon. It was a logical historical response because the powers these people had meant *their* actions were the most significant. By contrast, the masses were acknowledged only as a force that had compelled the main players to make certain decisions. For example, Nicholas II had taken the decision to create a *Duma*. He had been influenced to do so by the general unrest, but the key factor in the event was Nicholas himself. Western scholars also criticised the overemphasis by Marxist historians on the role of the proletariat, which they argued was small and insignificant. Far from being the first heroic effort of communist-inspired workers, the 1905 Revolution was more like a peasant rebellion. Moreover, the Marxists tended to exaggerate Lenin's 'genius' for predicting events. Liberal historians pointed out that Lenin was forced to reconsider the role of the peasantry in his thinking; such was their importance in the events of 1905. Lenin arrogantly clung to the belief that the proletariat, led by a revolutionary guard, would effect a revolution, but Lenin had nagging doubts, after the dismal performance of the workers and the central role played by the peasants. Marxists never acknowledged this doubt, stressing the 'inevitability' of the proletarians success, in accordance with their rigid ideology.

The libertarian (Western, left-wing) view focused on the people

Libertarians were unimpressed by the emphasis on leaders when it appeared obvious to them that the revolution had been carried out by the broad mass of the people. It was unimportant that the 1905 Revolution had failed to achieve much; what was significant was that so many Russians had expressed their anger and discontent, and had taken their destinies into their own hands. This was an outburst by 'ordinary people', who were sick of their conditions and their immediate overlords. There was a certain romance about this viewpoint, and it was not dissimilar from the Marxist notion of heroic failure. E.P. Thompson had captured the imagination by his book *The Making of the English Working Class* (1963) in which he argued that far from being inert victims of economic forces unleashed by the industrial revolution, the proletariat were capable of revolt. Moreover, he argued that there was a working class in existence before the industrial revolution and it was this class that had sometimes opposed the progress of capitalism. Thompson argued that it did not matter that they failed, since they were still worthy of study. His great contribution to history was that he reminded scholars not to become slaves to an ideologically driven formula, as the Marxists had been. Translated to Russian history, this means that previous accounts had been wrong to concentrate only on economics and leaders; there should be room for the myriad responses of different social groups and nationalities to the 1905 Revolution.

The revisionists weigh up the relative importance of factors
The chief problem with the libertarian perspective is that there is a risk of exaggerating the importance, or the significance, of the lower classes who had little influence over the decisions taken or of the outcomes. Therefore a historian who wanted to know why the 1905 Revolution turned out as it did would be misled if they spent all their time looking into the actions and opinions of workers and peasants. Where the Marxists had given too much weight to the early Bolshevik movement in their histories, so the libertarians risked overemphasising the role of the people. A more accurate, and less ideologically-loaded viewpoint, is to weigh up the relative importance of the people, the decision-makers and the situation. There was no attempt to overthrow the Tsar; at best there was a desire to force Nicholas II into moderate concessions. Nicholas II did, however, make some concessions because of the violence in the countryside and in the towns. With many of his regiments committed to the Far East, where they were facing defeat, he lacked the means to deal with the revolt. He attempted to buy time against the opposition with the creation of a *Duma*, but he was insincere and undermined it as soon as his troops had regained control. His failure to tackle adequately the grievances of the people stored up problems for the future. Thus, the relative importance of each group is identified and acknowledged.

The consequences of Tsarist Foreign policy, 1905–14

Russia's imperial expansion was checked
The limits of Russia's imperialistic ambitions were defined in the late-nineteenth

century after 300 years of gradual expansion eastwards across Siberia. A series of wars in the second half of the nineteenth century secured Central Asia, but the British control of much of the Middle East and South Asia prevented further annexations. Russia sold Alaska to the United States in 1867, and the development of the Far Eastern port of Vladivostok was dependent on the completion of the Trans-Siberian Railway. However, this new development aroused the hostility of Japan, who feared that Korea would be the next to be annexed. Russia confirmed this suspicion when it compelled the Japanese to relinquish the Laiotung Peninsula after the Sino-Japanese War of 1894–95, only to seize the land for itself in 1898. When Mongolia and Manchuria fell under Russian influence at the turn of the century, the Japanese prepared for a lightning war.

The Russo-Japanese War ended in the defeat of Russian expansionism

The Japanese launched a surprise attack on Port Arthur in 1904 to neutralise the Russian Pacific Fleet. After a long siege, the port fell. Russia had immense difficulties reinforcing its Far Eastern garrison as all the troops and supplies had to pass along the Trans-Siberian Railway. As in the Crimean War, Russia was finding it difficult to fight a war on the very periphery of the empire because of poor logistics and transport. The Japanese forced the army of General Kuropatkin to withdraw after a major battle at Mukden (February–March 1905). To cut the Japanese supply routes, the Russians despatched the Baltic Fleet right round the world, but its well-publicised voyage ended in May 1905 when it was ambushed by Admiral Togo's main battle fleet in the Tsushima Strait. The Russians lost 25 out of their 35 vessels to highly trained Japanese gunners.

The war created new ambitions for Russia and its rivals

With growing unrest at home, the Russians were relieved by an American offer of mediation which resulted in the Treaty of Portsmouth. Russia had been humiliated and its apparent weakness fuelled German and Austrian geopolitical ambitions. Germany's Kaiser pursued a policy of 'Weltpolitik' (seeking to increase Germany's global influence), whilst Austria, hoping to crush Slav nationalism, annexed Bosnia in 1908. However, the Russians were more determined than ever to restore their national honour and they sought to challenge Austrian arrogance in the Balkans. This led to unmitigated support for Serbia in 1914. Serbians were seen as 'fellow Slavs' and co-religionists; they were also useful allies in the drive to secure a Russian-dominated Balkans. However, the Serbian government used its Russian backing to pursue a dangerous policy against Austria. Although the Serbian government knew that assassins planned to murder the heir to Austrian throne, they failed to stop them. They were guilty of aiding a terrorist organisation, but they refused to be coerced by the Austrians when a harsh ultimatum arrived from Vienna. When Austrian troops began to march towards the Russian borders, as well as the Serbian frontier, the Tsar ordered the mobilisation of the Russian army. This prompted Germany to begin its own mobilisation and the instantaneous implementation of its war plan. The First World War had begun and it was greeted with rapturous enthusiasm in St Petersburg. It was not to last.

Russia and the First World War

The years immediately before the war

The Tsar was determined to continue autocratic rule by reducing the powers of the *Duma* and harnessing the new capitalist economy. The *Duma* managed to pass legislation to improve the literacy of peasants, but it was not enough. The agricultural reforms stood little chance of producing loyal, conservative, capitalist farmers. Most land enclosures were by the communes not by individuals, the low productivity continued, there was a rise in the rural population and there was an acute land hunger. In urban areas, there were still no trade unions, and there was a growing political consciousness, and class division. Social calm in the cities had a bleak outlook. This worried the liberals who were caught between the seething masses on one side and an immobile Tsar on the other. They began to lose faith in the *Duma*. In the period 1912–1914, a wave of strikes indicated the depth of unrest.

Year	Numbers of strikers
1905	c.3,000,000
1906	1,000,000
1907	400,000
1908	174,000
1909	64,000

Once again the revolutionaries were left behind

The workers were not co-ordinated. There was one particularly bloody incident at the Lena goldfields where the army shot down strikers. It showed that the regime had fully recovered from the 1905 fiasco. The fact that the numbers of strikers was falling also shows that it was becoming more dangerous to act. The revolutionaries were demoralised. Their numbers fell from 100,000 in 1905 to 10,000 in 1909. Many were in exile, like the Bolsheviks and Mensheviks. Many were inactive and even proactive ones like Lenin were engaged in theoretical debate rather than firm action. The death of Stolypin saw a brief rise in the number of strikes (2,000 in 1912).

The Tsarist regime welcomed the outbreak of the First World War

Tsarist ministers believed the war would generate a feeling of patriotism that would crush the ideas of revolution. Revolutionaries felt that the war would seriously disrupt the path to revolution. Yet Witte, who died in 1914, warned that the war would bring dangers for the Tsar. Lenin too believed the war might serve the revolutionary purpose if the discontent it would generate could be harnessed and exploited. Trotsky later remarked that 'war is the locomotive of change'. Unlike the war of 1904–5, the world war was a conflict of greater scale and duration. It would involve larger numbers of civilians than the Russo-Japanese War too. It prevented a solution to the country's political problems (thus alienating the liberals and revolutionaries) and its socio-economic problems (angering the peasants and workers). Most important of all, it caused the defeat of the army and therefore deprived the regime of its instrument of control. Economically, the war caused a dislocation of the country and diverted much needed resources. When the Tsar took charge of the war effort, he made himself personally liable for failure.

The Russian invasion of East Prussia in 1914 was badly executed

The German 8th Army was ordered to hold the Russians in the east, but the Austrian forces in Galicia decided not to depend on German co-operation, and advanced into Poland. The Russians were therefore prompted to take offensive action earlier than expected, but this was also because the French, enduring the onslaught of the main German attack, were pleading for a diversion. There was little coherence in the Russian offensive, except a vague intention to advance on Berlin and Vienna. Russian troops were also inadequately supplied and their horse-drawn transport was confined to narrow roads. General Pavel Rennen-kampf began his attack on the Germans in East Prussia by establishing one army at Gumbinnen and a second army south of the Masurian Lakes. However, the distances between the armies meant that co-ordination and mutual support was impossible. Worse, the commander of the Second Army, General Aleksandr Samsonov, was a personal enemy of Rennenkampf. The Battle of Tannenburg that followed on 26–29 August 1914 was a disaster for the Russians. They were enveloped and compelled to surrender en masse. Ninety thousand were taken prisoner, 30,000 Russians had become casualties and 500 guns had been captured in the first weeks of the war.

The war in the east continued to go badly for Russia

The Austrians continued to penetrate Poland (whilst the Germans fought the Russians to a standstill at Tannenburg), but the Russians checked the Austrians near their own border. The huge distances meant that fighting on the eastern front didn't remain as static as in the west. Cavalry and mounted infantry continued to play a key role in reconnaissance, or as screens for troop movements. The Germans, thwarted in the west, decided to switch more troops to the eastern theatre during 1915. The Austrians also managed to crack Russian codes early on which gave them an advantage if they obtained any radio or telephone traffic. Still hoping to exploit their numerical advantage, Russian commanders poured troops into headlong attacks against the Germans and Austrians. One Austrian machine gunner recalled firing his machine gun constantly into Russian infantry swarming towards his position. So many were killed, that he and his comrades had to periodically run forward and clear the heaps of bodies from in front of their trenches so as to maintain a field of fire. Russian soldiers were undoubtedly brave, but there would be a limit to this endurance in the face of such attrition.

The failure of the Russian army led directly to the collapse of Russia

In 1916, General Alexei Brusilov launched a well-organised and gigantic offensive against two Austrian armies near Czernowitz. It was so successful that the Germans were forced to divert troops to assist the Austrians. When the Russians reached the Carpathian Mountains, exhaustion, lack of supplies and one million casualties halted the attack. The failure of Brusilov broke the army's will, although it continued to function into 1917. Conditions in the Russian army were generally so poor, and food so scarce at home, that the people and reserves of the army in Petrograd (renamed from the German 'St Petersburg' to sound more patriotic) revolted in February 1917.

Analysis of the Russian army

▶ The Russian army performed quite well to begin with and it survived until 1917 against Europe's best; the German army and their Austrian allies. It lacked the equipment and training to make it effective but morale was high. Supply problems were to some extent inevitable given the vast distances involved, the width of the front and the state of the Russian infrastructure. In some cases, troops received no winter clothing despite freezing conditions. In another instance, soldiers discovered their rations consisted of barrels of worm-ridden, rotting fish.

▶ The Russians got into the war quicker than anticipated and they assisted the Allied war effort by dividing the Germans on two fronts.

▶ The Russians suffered very heavy casualties. Thirty-seven per cent of Russian men were called up during the war. The official figure was 1,700,000 dead but, according to Correlli Barnett, it is likely to have been double that.

▶ The Russian army suffered a string of defeats, which caused a loss of faith in the officers. The Russian army had not yet begun to fragment. Norman Stone dismissed the idea as 'a Bolshevik fabrication', for mass desertions didn't really begin until late 1917, although there had been a small but steady trickle before. Moreover, the revolution did not begin at the front, it began amongst soldiers assailed by rumours and scare stories back in St Petersburg.

The economic effects of the war

▶ Russia was not equipped for a modern, total war. Production rose but not as fast as in Germany. In 1914, Russia suffered shortages of guns and ammunition. This was not unusual perhaps (Britain had the same problem in 1914–15) but Russia lacked the industrial potential that the powers in the West enjoyed. Industry made the transition to war painfully slowly. Foreign supplies were hard to get through: Russia was cut off by Germany, Austria and Turkey, and its ports were ice bound for half the year. Nevertheless, the latent potential of Russian industry, which was to be developed so spectacularly later by Stalin, was already evident: by late 1916, Russia exceeded German shell production.

▶ Railways were inadequate when placed under the demands of war. The volume, workload and distances were simply too great. Rails wore out and locomotives and rolling stock were not replaced. Extra goods had to be moved, including foreign coal, munitions and reserves, as well as troops, baggage, guns and supplies. In 1914, there were 20,000 locomotives, but in 1917 this had fallen to 9,000. Before the war there had been 500,000 rolling stock, but in 1917 this was down to 174,000. In the winter of 1916–17, one of the most severe of the century, 1,200 locomotives burst their boilers.

▶ In the cities, food and fuel supplies were erratic and then dried up. J.N. Westwood (*Endurance and Endeavour, Russian History 1812–1980*) is surprised the Russian people endured these conditions for as long as they did. Civilians suffered as much as the troops. War weariness set in.

▶ Inflation sent prices up. Wages fell in real terms.

▶ Peasants were able to sell their produce direct to the cities, if they were near one.

A comparison of 1905 and the effects of the war

The war intensified to breaking point the existing stresses in society, politics and the economy. It deepened the gulf between all classes and produced a civil war. In summary this was due to:

▶ Defeats (like 1905).

▶ Failure to mobilise internal resources for total war (unlike 1905).

▶ The ruin of the gentry (accelerated by the war, but a process that had already begun).

▶ The rapid rise in heavy industry caused a shortage in housing, food and other consumer industries. (Already evident in 1905 but made more acute by the war.)

▶ Casualties, defeats, and lack of weapons, food and equipment undermined the loyalty of the army. (The army had been largely loyal in 1905.)

▶ A wave of strikes paralysed the economy and the government.

▶ Political groups were united by a common complaint: the Tsar. (This was new, since, in 1905, most were loyal to Nicholas II.)

Tutorial

Progress questions
1. What was the significance of the 1905 Revolution?
2. Which were the three most significant reasons for the failure of the 1905 Revolution?
3. Why, if Russia had suffered such disastrous consequences of defeat in 1905, did the regime welcome another war in 1914?
4. How significant were the economic changes caused by the First World War?

Discussion points
1. Could the 1905 Revolution, or indeed the 1917 Revolution, have been averted?
2. Why were the Russian leaders unsuccessful in finding a solution to the country's problems?

Practical assignment
Create a table listing the changes wrought by the First World War and compare them with the long-term changes taking place in Russia. Use this as a summary guide. Annotate onto the table the proposed solutions of the regime and of revolutionaries. What similarities and differences are there in their approaches?

Study tips
1. The key areas of this topic so far are the ideas of Lenin (Chapter 3), the failure of Tsarist economic reform (Chapter 2) and the growth of revolutionary unrest (this chapter). Your own notes and reading could be clustered around these topics.
2. Note how the Soviet interpretation of the 1905 Revolution differed from the accounts in the West. Be careful not to attribute too much importance to 'inevitability' or the 'proletariat', as the propagandists of the USSR played these up. This does not mean that they are necessarily 'wrong', but one needs to see them in context and in proportion. The Bolsheviks were still a small and almost unknown party in Russia. They had no power and the proletariat did not support them. Remember, all the revolutionaries, except many of the SRs, felt the peasantry had no role to play, but this was an error.
3. Be clear about the definitions of 'revolution': this is a favoured question.

5

The February Revolution and the Provisional Government

One-minute summary – The February Revolution was a spontaneous, popular outburst of anger at the terrible conditions thrown up by the war, all of which lay on top of existing economic and social problems. The successor regime was to be a democratically elected republic. However, until elections could be held, little progress could be made on reform, and there could not be elections until the war had turned in Russia's favour. Few imagined that Russia, unburdened now the inept Tsar had gone, could not now win the war. So the struggle went on, but this fatal delay and the compounded miseries it brought eventually brought the provisional government into disrepute. Some have speculated that the provisional government was 'doomed to failure from the start' because, as Lionel Kochan put it, it failed to 'pour new wine into old skins'. However, it is debatable that the fall of the government was inevitable, and it is highly questionable to suggest that Lenin's victory in October 1917 was in any way a foregone conclusion.

In this chapter you will learn:

▶ the nature of the February Revolution
▶ theories on the February Revolution
▶ what measures the provisional government took and the problems they faced
▶ the Bolsheviks' position in 1917
▶ the July Days
▶ the Kornilov affair
▶ historical debates about this period.

The nature of the February Revolution

The spark of revolution

▶ In 1915, the Tsar dissolved the *Duma* because of its criticism of him and his running of the war effort. Alexandra the Tsarina also dismissed a series of prime ministers to please the court favourite Rasputin. Four prime ministers, three defence ministers and six ministers of the interior were sacked, but nothing improved. Rumours circulated that the Tsarina was a German spy and Rasputin an evil genius who was leading Russia to catastrophe. Edward Crankshaw wrote: 'Under Rasputin, fools and imbeciles were in charge...Russia rotted away from the centre, outside inwards until the shell fell in'. Rasputin was murdered in a 'court *coup*', but the disasters went on.

The collapse, when it came, took everyone by surprise. Lenin was writing, as late as 1916, that there would be no revolution in Russia in his lifetime.

▶ On 27 February (8 March by the old Russian, Gregorian calendar), a bread riot and a strike at the Putilov arms works coincided with a march by women (it was Women's Day) to create a combined demonstration. The unrest spread rapidly across the city, picking up its own momentum. The Tsar was alarmed by the slogans of the mob and proposed to return to the capital to crush the demonstrators.

▶ The Tsar was told to abdicate by his exasperated generals. They regarded his war leadership as Russia's greatest burden and refused to support action against the people in the capital. As the Tsar travelled back to Petrograd to take command, his aides and courtiers gradually left him. His brother, Grand Duke Michael, simply refused to take over. The *Duma* officials, seizing their moment, declared that the Tsar was overthrown. Tsarism therefore dissolved.

▶ The Revolution spread from Petrograd to rural areas. The peasants started to seize land. There was wild rejoicing throughout Russia and the French revolutionary anthem, the Marseillaise, was sung in Petrograd.

Freedoms when centralisation was needed
One of the first acts of the provisional government had been to grant liberal freedoms, such as freedom of speech and an amnesty for all political prisoners, but this was in stark contrast to western governments who were temporarily suspending civil liberties to safeguard public morale and a united war effort. The government stalled the resolution of the land question, knowing that peasant soldiers would be anxious about missing out on any redistribution of the land, and promises of an election were also delayed (until November 1917), so the new government had raised expectations without being able to deliver any substantial improvements.

Lenin returned in a German train
Lenin was not in Russia when the Revolution began, but he obtained the support of the German government in his desire to hurry to Petrograd. The Germans provided Lenin with a sealed train, that is to say it was not permitted to stop inside German territory, to convey Lenin and his Bolshevik colleagues immediately to Russia. A document exists which shows Lenin's signature, agreeing to the conditions laid down by the Germans. Lenin hoped to mobilise his party in Russia for an immediate seizure of power against the 'bourgeois' provisional government. He still clung to his belief, expressed in 1902, that a revolutionary elite was all that was needed.

Key points about this period

▶ The Tsar abdicated, but the monarchy could have survived if Grand Duke Michael had accepted the throne.

▶ The Tsar had lost the *means* and the *will* to resist (initially he wanted to resist but the generals abandoned him). This was in contrast to the 1905 Revolution. People blamed the Tsar for the new hardships. Opposition was united against him.

▶ The Revolution developed its own momentum. Despite the existence of revolutionary groups, there is no evidence of any planning.

▶ The *Duma* officials created a constitutional republic. They were unelected but formed a 'caretaker' government until elections could be held. First, the war had to be won.

▶ The Bolsheviks, once Lenin returned (courtesy of the Germans) worked to undermine the provisional government. He argued the revolution had not yet come. The Mensheviks were prepared to wait until conditions were right to overthrow the bourgeoisie and were prepared to co-operate with the *Duma* in the short term to alleviate the conditions of the workers and the peasants. Lenin wanted the two revolutions in one and no co-operation with the *Duma*.

▶ The Bolsheviks were small in number: barely 10,000. This suited Lenin who wanted a revolutionary elite to lead the proletariat. The primary objective was to win over the Petrograd *Soviet*. The bulk of the provisional government were middle class, but the *Soviets* were made up of workers, soldiers, sailors and some revolutionaries. Lenin wanted to use this to maintain a class division and claim legitimacy for his party.

Theories on the Revolution

1. The Bolsheviks (*Soviet* view)

According to the Marxists' viewpoint, the Bolsheviks had encouraged the revolution and foresaw it. Bolsheviks were amongst the leaders of the agitation and unrest. It was a proletarian victory, which, as expected, the bourgeoisie hijacked for their own ends. The workers were confident of final victory and knew this was a stage they had to pass through. The proletariat established their own *Soviets* (councils) with which they would seize power later.

▶ However, the Bolsheviks were scattered; Lenin was in Switzerland and was only alerted by the newspapers, Trotsky was in the USA, Stalin was in Siberia. The chances of the revolution being planned by the Bolsheviks seem remote. It is possible to see the proletariat as being the main actors in the drama, for it was their demonstration that sparked events, but the key *decisions* were taken by the generals and by the *Duma* officials.

2. The Katkov conspiracy theory

G. Katkov, a Liberal historian, believed the whole Revolution was secretly organised by the Germans. This seems absurd unless one considers that:

▶ The Germans were anxious to get Russia out of the war before the Americans joined (February 1917).

▶ Germany *did* benefit from the revolution, turning its efforts to the West.

▶ No clues would be left, except by agents.

▶ Lenin *was* returned to Russia by a German 'sealed train' to end Russia's part in the war. Germany got a favourable treaty in March 1918.

3. Pessimists (liberal)

The pessimist viewpoint expressed the idea that the revolution was inevitable because of Russia's conditions: it was just a question of when. The accumulation of grievances from before the war, and the awful conditions thrown up by the war, combined to drive the Russian people to demonstrations and rioting. The regime lacked the capacity to deal with the enormous problems Russia faced. This is reinforced by the fact that the provisional government was also unable to solve Russia's problems, and the country continued to disintegrate. The logical result was the collapse of authority, economic meltdown and civil war. Once the old system had entirely broken up, a new regime could emerge. Invariably after such chaos, revolutions spawn dictatorships.

4. Optimists (liberal)

In the optimists' view, the Revolution of 1917 could have been averted. It was the special problems thrown up by the war, and the compounding of old ones, which made the revolution occur, but if the pre-war Tsarist policies had been given more time, they would have worked. Russia could have moved gradually into a democratic system, with or without a monarchy. The war produced such a drastic dislocation of the economy that traditional authority broke up. When the system collapsed, the country was hijacked by a revolutionary organisation that destroyed democracy. But for the war, and the Bolsheviks, Russia may have prospered like the rest of Europe.

5. Accidental theory (accepted liberal view)

The revolution was not planned but began accidentally, spontaneously and gained momentum. Kochan wrote: 'It began in a small way; spontaneous, almost, one might say, unpolitically.' Food was the demand, not a change in politics, when the demonstrators hit the streets in February 1917. In fact, the fear of shortages was greater than the actual hardship they faced. Anthony Wood endorses this view, showing how anxieties and expectations initiated action by the people. The Petrograd garrison joined the demonstrators, for example, because they thought they were about to be sent to the Front. Others exploited the situation, and this pattern was repeated across the country.

6. The libertarian view

The emphasis of the libertarian perspective is on the role of ordinary people. Lenin is shown to be irrelevant compared with the importance of the masses in initiating and sustaining the revolution. The real revolution, outside of Petrograd, began in February and continued throughout the year. The protest against the terrible conditions found its expression in the Soviets, an explicit piece of evidence that the Russian people were capable of organising themselves without Bolshevik or liberal leadership. Without the efforts of the people, there would have been no Revolution, and Lenin was forced to tailor his ambitions to the needs of the people.

7. Military history

The army's loyalty was crucial to the outcome of the February Revolution. Without the army throwing in its lot with the demonstrators in Petrograd, Russia may have degenerated into a repeat of the 1905 Revolution, or worse, into a civil war. It was the war that compounded problems and brought the people to breaking point. Whilst it was the generals who made the February Revolution possible, later in the year the soldiers and sailors were the key 'revolutionary force' that determined events.

8. The revisionist view

The revisionists would suggest that Lenin was unimportant outside his own party at this stage, although he was to assume greater importance in the autumn of 1917. To understand the February Revolution, one has to weigh up the relative importance of all the factors. Clearly, the decision-makers were important. Prince Lvov, who took over the provisional government, made a critical judgement when he decided to grant civil liberties at the very moment the economy was collapsing under the strain of total war. However, without the involvement of the Petrograd crowds, it is unclear if and when the *Duma* officials would have summoned the courage to challenge Nicholas II. See Figure 2.

The provisional government: policies and problems

Continuing the war proved the undoing of the provisional government

Although the majority of Russians felt that, now the Tsar had gone, Russia could go on and win the war, the publication of the government's war aims, which included territorial annexation, angered many who felt the war should be one of

---

Long-term causes
- ▶ Tsar: unwilling to give up absolute power or to make concessions to the *Duma*. Often an indecisive character.
- ▶ The regime: repressive, corrupt, inefficient. Prestige damaged by the Bloody Sunday shootings and the Lena Goldfields 'massacre'.
- ▶ Middle classes: aspirations to govern.
- ▶ Urban workers: angry at their conditions.
- ▶ Peasants: poverty, land hunger, resentment at land owners, forced to leave the land to occupy poor accommodation and accept low wages in the cities.

Short-term causes (the war)
- ▶ Defeats and casualties: soldiers and officers disaffected.
- ▶ Tsar: took personal command at the Front and was blamed for failures. Scandalous behaviour of Rasputin ruined the prestige of the monarchy.
- ▶ Middles classes: impatient with the inefficiency of the war effort and the Tsar's leadership.
- ▶ Economic effects of the war: food shortages, prices inflated, fuel shortages, breakdown of vital rail system, food production falling as peasants conscripted.
- ▶ Failure of the Brusilov Offensive (1916): prompted unrest in Petrograd and the generals urged the Tsar to abdicate.
- ▶ Workers in Petrograd: anger at the conditions (prices, hours and shortages) initiated strikes and demonstrations. Popularity of protests grew encouraging the *Duma* to demand Tsar's abdication.

Figure 2. Causes of the February 1917 Revolution.

self-defence against Germany and not a resurrection of Tsarist adventures. The war proved the undoing of the government. All the problems associated with the war, such as shortages, defeats, losses, and high prices, continued and were magnified. The army had formed *Soviets* (councils), and, encouraged by the publication of a Bolshevik-inspired document, Soviet Order No. 1, discipline collapsed over a period of several months. The provisional government appointed Brusilov the Chief of Staff, but the failure of his second offensive in 1917 (1–19 July) marked the total collapse of the Russian army. Russian soldiers gradually deserted in droves. Whole regiments gave up. Men shot their officers to avoid combat. Looting of stores and alcohol rendered them unfit to offer any resistance to the advancing Germans. The disintegration took place over a long period of time and did not affect all units. Many units that had remained intact during this period fought throughout the civil war of 1918–20.

The key issues of March 1917
The provisional government was faced by a number of immediate problems. It had already been decided to continue the war in the hope that co-operation with the Allies would secure the return of territory lost to the Germans and ensure co-operation after the war. The second problem was the economy. The supply of food

and fuel had to be improved in the short term, and the government was assisted by many of the workers themselves who settled agreements with their employers quickly. Employers seemed willing to conclude agreements to avoid trouble with the workforce. The wider issue of social reform needed addressing. It was unclear how far improved working conditions could be effected while the war was still on, and changes to living conditions was a gigantic problem that would take years to solve. In the countryside, the government had to decide whether land should be taken from landowners and redistributed. Most of the provisional government favoured the principle of private property, but it was a complex issue that needed time. Land could not be distributed fairly when peasants were still serving at the Front. Finally, the national minorities would be demanding independence or autonomy within the old empire, so the government would have to decide what concessions could be granted in wartime. Essentially a united anti-German front was preferred.

The provisional government and the *Soviets*

The *Soviets* (councils) of workers, peasants, soldiers and sailors had been springing up across the country after the February Revolution in various sizes. The *Soviets* tended to run the public services (water, food distribution, roads, communications) and the provisional government was the accepted national decision-making body. In this sense, both the *Soviets* and the provisional government needed each other. In one sense, the war effort united them, but as the year wore on and shortages got worse, the war eroded the goodwill. Decisions made by the provisional government in July and September also affected the relationship.

The provisional government was not at loggerheads with the *Soviet* at first

Prince Lvov and a group of *Duma* officials, augmented with members of left wing parties, initially led the Provisional government. Although *Soviet* historians later tried to claim that the workers', soldiers' and sailors' *Soviets* were opposed to the provisional government from the outset because of their class differences, there is no evidence of this. Indeed, Alexander Kerensky, who succeeded Lvov, was actually the chairman of the Petrograd *Soviet*. The government became unpopular for its policies gradually during 1917.

The polices of the liberals and socialists

The provisional government was dominated by the Kadets (Constitutional Democrats). Their leader, Milyukov, felt that the February Revolution had achieved its aim of establishing a constitutional government and that further change would lead to anarchy. The Kadets favoured a democratic but centralised state. Left-wing members of the Kadets believed that further reform was necessary, and that more power should be devolved to regions and local governments (although even the left wing of the Kadets did not want to see the old empire broken up). The Kadets were united, though, on continuing the war, and Milyukov served as War Minister. They were prepared to delay the redistribution of the land until a democratically elected assembly could be formed. Holding an election during the miserable conditions of the war was unlikely to help them, but a victory would, so elections were also delayed. Socialists, strongly represented by the SRs and by a handful of Mensheviks, were prepared to co-operate with the provisional government to ensure their demands were met. The moderate SRs, including their leader Chernov, tolerated the idea of continuing the war to defend Russian territory, a view nicknamed 'Revolutionary Defencism', but some felt the war should be stopped as soon as possible. The Mensheviks were also split, with Martov and the Menshevik-Internationalists against war, and Tsereteli and Moderate Mensheviks for it. On land, there was a desire to redistribute land as soon as possible, although the war was recognised as an obstacle to this. It was felt that national minorities should be granted autonomy; Ukraine was to have immediate self-government.

The Bolshevik position

Lenin was in difficulties

When Lenin returned, some regarded him as inspirational, but his call for an immediate revolution was not popular throughout the party. When Lenin demanded a revolutionary elite, his party reminded him that, if they were to take power, they would need mass, popular backing. Lenin appealed to the Petrograd *Soviet*, ordering them to follow him into power, but he was ridiculed. Lenin's speeches seemed sarcastic and patronising compared with Kerensky's effective and fiery oratory. Rumours began to circulate that Lenin was a German spy, sent by the Kaiser to undermine the Russian war effort. Soviet historians later concealed these facts. They rewrote the events of March–October as one continuous round of successes for Lenin. They claimed he had planned everything, was immensely popular and predicted accurately all that would take place. The only obstacle, they argued, was the presence of counter-revolutionaries (a convenient excuse to rid themselves of opponents later when they were in power).

The April Theses and Bolshevik propaganda were misleading

In the April Theses, published after Lenin's return to Russia, Lenin put forward a slogan of 'Peace, Bread and Land'.

▶ He argued for immediate peace with Germany. This was initially unpopular, but after the failure of the July 1917 offensive, and the decay of the army, people were more prepared to listen. The miseries caused by the war made this a popular cause.

▶ The 'Land' slogan was more problematic. Lenin wanted the nationalisation of land to end private property. This was deeply unpopular. The peasants wanted their own land and the peasants were still the majority of the country. As the peasants began to seize the land anyway, regardless of the policy of the provisional government, Lenin pretended to go along with it and stated 'Land – for the people' (this had the double meaning of land for individual people or common ownership by all the people, that is, the abolition of individual ownership).

▶ The slogan 'Bread' was also popular as everyone, regardless of class or background, was hungry. It seemed to be the greatest priority.

▶ To win over the Soviets, Lenin adopted another slogan: 'All Power to the Soviets'. This was another insincere statement. Lenin meant to have a revolutionary elite in charge, strictly disciplined. He felt that popular support was irrelevant in seizing power. However, for practical reasons he couldn't act without them, and the slogan made it seem he was the champion of ordinary people. His objective was power for his small party, so that a new communist order could be imposed. Propaganda should not obscure our analysis of Lenin's true aims.

The July Days

There was growing dissatisfaction with the provisional government

The provisional government was deeply unpopular when it was revealed that Milyukov, the Minister of War, secretly wanted to pursue expansionist war aims instead of a simple defence of Russian soil. Protests from the *Soviets* led to the formation of a new coalition of socialists and liberals on 5 May 1917. The Menshevik leader, Tsereteli, and the SR leader, Chernov, were amongst the five socialists now in government. The problem was that this tied the moderate socialists to the provisional government; any mistakes would now discredit the moderate Left.

The July Days failed to change the leadership of Russia

When conditions worsened during the summer of 1917, soldiers and workers grew disillusioned. News that another offensive had failed led to demonstrations and eventually to rioting on 3 July, the first of the so-called 'July Days'. Sailors from Kronstadt, 20,000 strong, arrived in Petrograd the next day and marched on the Tauride Palace, the seat of the provisional government. They demanded that the *Soviets* take power and they almost lynched Chernov in the streets. Troops loyal to the provisional government arrived later and, on the 5th, protesting workers and the extremist agitators in Petrograd were shot down. This incident played into the hands of the government's opponents as a propaganda scoop, but a letter was published showing how Lenin was in the pay of the Germans. The letter suggested that Lenin had been sent to undermine the Russian war effort. Many Bolsheviks were arrested and imprisoned, and many Russians, including the members of the Petrograd *Soviet*, condemned Lenin. The rising, if it had ever been one, had failed.

Lenin showed little leadership in the July Days

Soviet historians tended to play down the importance of the July Days, but if it was acknowledged at all, it was shown how Lenin's leadership was crucial to the success of the revolution. For when the Kronstadt sailors marched into Petrograd on 4 July 1917, Lenin was on holiday in Finland. He returned but urged restraint and his Central Committee called off a planned demonstration for the 5th. Despite Lenin's usual assertions that the party should seize power, he made no move and decided to see what would happen. This was hardly the decisive leadership of *Soviet* myth. The failure of the rising and the provisional government's arrests of leading Bolsheviks forced Lenin to scuttle back to Finland in disguise. *Soviet* historians gave the undignified escape a veneer of heroism by focussing on Lenin's writings, the humbleness of his surroundings and the harsh response of the provisional government. The government was condemned as 'bourgeois', fit only to be overthrown, even though it contained revolutionary Marxists. Edward Acton accounted for Lenin's attitude towards the July Days as a party problem. It was not the disciplined organisation that Lenin had envisaged back in 1902, but a movement that sometimes acted without Lenin's direction. As membership of the party grew, so activists created their own cells and held their own meetings. Rumours circulated rapidly, and directives from the party leadership were sometimes deliberately ignored. As Robert Service points out, although Lenin had tried to limit party membership in the early days, his own rank and file demanded that the party become a mass movement.

The Kornilov affair

Kerensky faced many problems as Prime Minister

Alexander Kerensky was appointed Prime Minister on 8 July 1917, but he faced a number of problems that worsened by the end of August:

▶ The liberals in the provisional government wanted to delay land reform, defend the existing property owners, restore military discipline in the armed forces and order on the streets.

▶ The moderate *Soviet* leaders were losing their influence because of their collaboration with the provisional government.

▶ The army was cracking up and indiscipline was widespread. Soldiers commandeered trains at will to get home, adding another burden to an already overstretched network.

▶ Peasants continued to seize land and violence was more common. Country houses were burned down, landlords murdered and robbery increased.

▶ Crime increased in the cities. Richer people were mugged and theft increased dramatically.

Kerensky's solution was to restore order and discipline using the army

Kerensky responded by calling on the country to continue the war against Germany. He could not conclude a negotiated peace because he would be branded a traitor, and because the Germans would extract a high price for peace (as they did later against the Bolsheviks). The economic situation was dire, but he could do nothing until the war was brought to a satisfactory conclusion. To restore order and to win victory in the field, he needed a new commander in chief. He selected General Kornilov.

Kerensky's reputation was damaged by the Kornilov *coup* attempt

However, in September 1917 the new head of the armed forces tired of the revolutionaries back in Petrograd, and he offered to march his 'Iron Division' into the city to restore order. Kerensky initially went along with the idea, convinced that rival factions, especially the Mensheviks and Bolsheviks, were preparing to attack the government. However, suspicions grew, fanned by Bolshevik propaganda, that he was about to side with Kornilov in a right wing *coup* attempt. Kerensky was, in fact, convinced that Kornilov meant to crush the revolutionaries *and* the government to impose his own dictatorship. Without any troops of his own, Kerensky appealed to all the people of Petrograd, including the revolutionaries, to assist in turning back Kornilov's troops. Frantic preparations were made for the defence of the city, but the Bolsheviks closed railway lines and infiltrated the Iron Division. When Kornilov woke one morning to continue his advance, he was arrested by his own men. Kerensky should have emerged more popular than ever for saving Petrograd, but the Bolsheviks' propaganda discredited the provisional government. Kerensky seemed to lose his will to govern at this stage. Rumours circulated that he was involved in a scandalous affair with his wife's cousin and that he was addicted to cocaine. Perhaps his addiction and his depression began to affect his judgement. By October, the government was thoroughly detested, but Kerensky believed he could easily crush the Bolsheviks. On 24 October 1917, he ordered that two Bolshevik newspapers be closed down and announced that he intended to act against the Bolshevik party. This gave the Bolsheviks the excuse that they were 'acting in self-defence' when, in fact, they were preparing to overthrow the government.

Historical debates

The myths about 1917 have been hard to expunge

There were many myths created by the Bolsheviks about 1917:

► Bolsheviks claimed to have mass support throughout the year. They didn't. They failed to gain power in July and they later lost the elections in November 1918. They had to fight a civil war in 1918–1920 to impose their views and abolished democracy (a system based on majority rule). It is true to say that their movement grew in numbers and that they attracted significantly more support by the autumn of 1917 compared with the spring of that year.

► Bolsheviks claimed to run the *Soviets*. Lenin tried to influence them, which was all he could do. He did not control them. Gradually many members lost interest and went home. The Bolsheviks were ordered to continue to attend and did so, gradually increasing the proportion of the membership. Their influence was therefore greater by the end of the year.

► The first Bolshevik *coup* was in July not in October, but it was a bungled effort. Lenin failed to persuade his party to take power in March (when he arrived in Russia), and failed to get power in July, when his party tried to jump on the bandwagon of workers' discontent. Lenin fled to Finland in disguise (some say he was dressed as a woman, other accounts have him dressed as a worker). Therefore, by the late summer of 1917, Lenin was back in exile, his party was scattered and many were in prison. If Lenin had died in August 1917, he would be regarded as a total failure. His party members were demoralised. They were saved by the Kornilov affair and by the greater unpopularity of the government.

► The October revolution was a great popular uprising, dwarfing the events of February 1917, the Soviet historians claimed. Skilful propaganda and a daring *coup* got them control of Petrograd. Brutal methods then followed to secure power. These will be examined in the next chapter.

The liberal and libertarian viewpoints

Although the *Soviet* historians played up Lenin's rise in popularity, liberal historians did not discount this, nor did they challenge the important role that Lenin played in the events leading up to October 1917. Once again, leaders and the events in Petrograd were the focus of historical interest. Libertarian historians, by contrast, pointed to the countryside and the process of revolutionary change taking place there. All over Russia, rural people were taking the land for themselves and loosely co-operating along the lines of the *Mirs*. They would tend to examine the meetings of ordinary people, in both urban and rural areas, rather than the exaggerated incidents in and around the capital.

The revisionist view

The revisionist view is to take stock of how Lenin was forced to adapt to events and to opportunities. The July Days were certainly a major setback, but Lenin worked hard to exploit the grievances of the people. The April Theses' slogans became better known and were more in tune with popular opinion in the capital than Kerensky's rather tired calls for the defence of Russia. Kerensky must also take the blame for some of the unpopular moves of the provisional government, and the Kornilov fiasco. Propaganda was certainly influential. Although they were still a small party, the Bolsheviks produced 40 newspapers! However, the libertarians were right to suggest that the rural population had been overlooked. It was there and in many small towns and cities across Russia that a real, and largely social, revolution was taking place.

Tutorial

Progress questions

1. What evidence is there to suggest the February Revolution was spontaneous and popular?
2. What were the provisional government's chief errors in 1917?
3. Why didn't Lenin take power in April 1917?
4. What were the effects of the Kornilov *coup* attempt?

Seminar discussion

What assessment can be made of Lenin's leadership qualities in the period 1914–1917?

Practical assignment

Create a table of three columns. The first should be labelled 'Problem', the second 'Government response' and the third 'How successful?' Use this chapter to identify the main issues facing the government and assess how well they dealt with the problems they faced. To what extent did the problems accumulate through their own errors, and how far were they events outside of the government's control? What credit should be given to Lenin for the fortunes of the government? Annotate answers to these questions beneath the table.

Study tips

1. Be aware of the myths about this period. Try to analyse each of the interpretations that have been offered. Assess the strengths and weaknesses of each one against the period February to October 1917.
2. Think about the question of 'inevitability' here with respect to revolutions and the later success of the Bolsheviks.
3. Note how the notion of the revolution became an idea each party or leader could invoke to justify their actions. Leaders would each claim to be

'defending the revolution' or 'acting in the name of the people'. Anyone who disagreed with them was denounced as a traitor, enemy of the people or counter-revolutionary, and this gave licence for opponents to be persecuted. This tactic became a common feature of communism.

6

The October Revolution

One-minute summary – Soviet historians later described the seizure of power by the Bolsheviks as a glorious moment in Russian history. They argued that the working classes expressed strong support for Lenin and his party. With a brave and disciplined revolutionary guard at their head, they swept into power. The reason for this success and the establishment of communism in Russia had been the combination of Lenin's leadership and the way in which Bolshevik ideology genuinely reflected the desires of the proletariat. Just as Marx and Lenin had predicted, the communists came to power through the irresistible will of the people. This version of events does not stand up to the evidence and owed more to communist propaganda than reality. Nevertheless, without access to the archives in Russia, it was difficult to be sure exactly what had happened. Before 1991, many left-wing historians in the West wanted to believe that the revolution had been a popular uprising and that it had been hijacked by the Bolsheviks. More recently, historians acknowledge the role that Lenin played, but also how far his decisions were shaped by events.

In this chapter you will learn:

▶ the realities and myths about the October Revolution
▶ the fate of the Constituent Assembly.

The October Revolution: myths and realities

Lenin decided to act against the government in October

After the Kornilov crisis, the provisional government was progressively less popular. Lenin, who had made a greater propaganda effort through speeches, newspapers, handbills and subversion in the armed forces, was concerned about the following factors:

▶ The elections for the constituent elections were imminent (November). The Bolsheviks would probably lose, as they did not have a majority.

▶ Elections for the Petrograd *Soviet* were imminent. These might be won by Social Revolutionaries or Mensheviks.

▶ Kerensky had been discredited and had no armed forces to support him.

▶ Bolshevik propaganda was beginning to have an effect. The Bolsheviks were promising 'Peace, Bread and Land', which was popular with all groups in

The Marxist view (the official line of the Soviet Union and foreign communists)	A popular uprising that was carried out by the urban proletariat, led by Lenin and his vanguard of Bolsheviks. The working classes established the Soviets which supported Lenin and became his power base in the country. Lenin took the critical decisions.
The liberal view (Western view common during the Cold War and held by Robert Conquest, Richard Pipes and Leonard Shapiro)	A tiny minority seized power and began imposing their will on others. Lenin was the architect of the system, but his leadership was a disaster, plunging the country into civil war.
The libertarian view (View held by left-leaning academics in the West, including Stephen Smith and Sheila Fitzpatrick)	A genuine mass movement of discontent of which the events in Petrograd were only a part. The rank and file of the Bolshevik Party had far more influence over events than just the leaders, however the Party was undisciplined and not always able to control what happened.
The revisionists (Chris Read, Robert Service)	Lenin was a key figure and he was a decision maker of some importance because of the changing circumstances he found himself in. The October Revolution was a *coup*, but local actions were important, both by members of the Party and the mass of the citizenry.
Other factors	The October Revolution was successful because the provisional government had failed to solve the country's problems. Kerensky lost credibility in the Kornilov affair, the country was being defeated in war, the economy was in a state of collapse and the traditional, respected authority (the Tsar) had been discredited and overthrown already.
Inevitable?	It is very doubtful that the October Revolution was inevitable, but it could be argued that action against Kerensky was very likely. The SRs won the Assembly Elections that followed, so it is possible that the SRs would have formed a new government.

Figure 3. The October Revolution.

Russia. They also claimed to have 'saved' Petrograd.

▶ The Germans were advancing on Petrograd and might capture the city before the winter was over.

▶ Another right-wing *coup* may be attempted, and succeed.

▶ Kerensky appeared to be about to order the arrest of all the Bolsheviks. Trotsky later made much of this fact, to argue the Bolsheviks were acting in self-defence.

The *coup* of October 1917

Kerensky simply could not find any troops that he could rely on to arrest the Bolsheviks and he fled the city in a car borrowed from the American Embassy. On the night of the 24–25 October, Trotsky's hastily-formed Military Revolutionary Committee (MRC) sent small detachments of Red Guards to take up positions on bridges, at the telegraph exchange, railways stations and power stations. The telegraph office was contested but there was no resistance elsewhere. The next morning, people went about their business and little seemed to have changed. In the afternoon, Bolshevik units were assembled in front of the Winter Palace but, as no one knew what was going on, nothing happened. Most of the government troops inside the Palace got drunk and deserted. At 2am on the 26th, on a signal fired by the gunboat *Aurora*, the Bolsheviks sent armed men, many of them disguised as provisional government troops, into the Winter Palace by the back entrances. At gunpoint, a handful of military cadets and the panic-stricken Women's Battalion were disarmed. On the 26th, the All-Russian Congress of *Soviets* met and immediately denounced the Bolsheviks' actions. The Bolsheviks were unrepresentative of the Russian people and had no right to seize control of Petrograd. The delegates of the Congress of *Soviets* were concerned that the Bolshevik action would precipitate a right-wing counter-attack, just at the point when the Russian people were beginning to accept social democracy. Trotsky replied that the Soviet should go 'where it ought to be – to the dustbin of history!' The socialists left the hall, and this gave the Bolsheviks a majority. Lenin arrived, declared a Bolshevik Government was now established and stated an intention to hand all land to the people and end the war.

The *Soviet* view of the October Revolution

The *Soviet* propagandists later 'rewrote' the events of October 1917 to fit in with a more heroic image. Far from the clandestine and quiet seizure of key installations and the Winter Palace, the communists claimed there had been a great battle involving thousands of people. They claimed the Bolsheviks had swept to power with overwhelming popular support. Sergei Eisenstein even made a film 'reconstructing' the storming of the Winter Palace with a gigantic gun battle and plenty of stirring choral music. The idea was to convince later generations of Russians, or those who had not been in Petrograd, that communism was truly popular and was the only real 'people's government'. All other forms of authority were condemned as 'bourgeois' and elitist, and the middle classes were 'parasites' and 'bloodsuckers'. The propaganda myth legitimised the rather grubby manner in which the Bolsheviks had really taken power. Lenin was portrayed as brave and in the vanguard of the revolution, rather than a distant decision-maker. Trotsky was the real architect of the coup, but he was 'removed' from the event by Stalin in the 1930s. Even the Soviet was recast as an enthusiastic agency in support of the Bolsheviks. No other historical interpretation was permitted in the Soviet Union.

There was anarchy at first

Far from popularity, the Bolsheviks faced a wave of protests and anarchy. Drunken soldiers and sailors went on a robbing spree in the richer districts of Petrograd, and looting broke out everywhere. Banks and other businesses complained about the Bolsheviks' actions, bombarding Lenin with petitions. When Trotsky turned up and declared himself in charge of the Ministry of Foreign Affairs, officials simply laughed and walked out. Unable to rule through the Petrograd *Soviet*, as everyone expected Lenin would have to do, the Bolshevik leader simply established a new body called *Sovnakom* which consisted entirely of Bolsheviks. As the protests mounted, only armed force could ensure Lenin got his wishes granted. The state banks were forced to open their vaults at bayonet point.

The Bolsheviks were faced with a number of faits accompli

After ten days of street fighting in Moscow, the Bolsheviks also secured a tenuous hold on power there, but in the countryside, there was indifference if not hostility. The Bolsheviks grandly declared that the peasants could take the land of the landowners and decide for themselves how it should be divided up. This was ironic because the peasants were already doing this, and it flew in the face of communist principles. Lenin wanted all the land to be held in common ownership, and prohibited from sale or rent. In the factories, the Bolsheviks declared that workers' committees could decide on production and finance, and they could 'supervise' the management. Workers took this to mean they could 'direct' their managers. The result was chaos. Some workers simply turned up and did nothing, but claimed their pay anyway. The Bolsheviks also declared self-determination for national minorities but since they did not control the areas in which the minorities lived, it was an empty statement: the minorities were declaring themselves independent. The Bolshevik strategy was to go along with the most popular polices for the time being so as to stay in power, even if it did not go along with their principles. Meanwhile, the Bolsheviks did their best to generate a fear and loathing of the bourgeoisie.

Bolshevism was characterised by brutality, crime and corruption

The second strand of the Bolshevik strategy was to assert their power gradually through a policy of terror. All non-Bolshevik press was banned in October. Leading opponents were murdered or imprisoned. On 7 December 1917, Lenin set up the Cheka, a secret police force that had authority to deal with any opposition in the most brutal way. Discipline was restored in the Bolshevik ranks as well as across their area of control. Criminal elements were especially attracted to an organisation that had licence to be violent or steal whatever it wanted. Already some Russians could spot an opportunity. Junior civil servants denounced their seniors and got instant promotion. The greater the enthusiasm exhibited for the new authorities, the greater one's chances of getting some reward. Atrocities were committed under the new banner of Bolshevism: Red Guards murdered 50 military cadets by throwing them one by one into the blast furnace of a steel factory.

The dissolution of the Constituent Assembly and destruction of the *Soviets*

Levels of protest at the Bolsheviks' behaviour could not be controlled entirely by force. The railwaymen's union, along with telegraph and postal workers, threatened to cut off Petrograd unless elections, promised by the provisional government, went ahead. Lenin reluctantly accepted this, but he deliberately sabotaged talks with other socialist parties and only accepted some SRs into the *Sovnakom* to give an impression of co-operation. The Bolsheviks were defeated in the elections (see table below), so Lenin immediately declared that his government represented a 'higher form of democracy' than an elected assembly. He declared it a 'bourgeois' institution. When the delegates met on 5 January 1918, they were surrounded by Red Guards, threatening to kill them. The Constituent Assembly adjourned, but when members tried to return, they found the doors guarded by the armed men. A crowd gathered to protest but it was fired on. Lenin declared it: 'the frank liquidation of democracy, by the idea of dictatorship'. Pedantically he went on: 'We shall now proceed to construct the socialist order'. In fact, the destruction of the Constituent Assembly was far more significant than the October 'revolution' because it was the end of democracy in Russia for 70 years. It was also the signal for widespread resistance to Bolshevik rule, and the civil war that followed cost the lives of millions of Russian people.

	Votes cast (millions)	Number of seats in the assembly	Percentage share of the vote
Social Revolutionaries	21.8	410	53
Bolsheviks	10	175	24
Kadets	2.1	17	5
Mensheviks	1.4	18	3
Others	6.3	62	15

The liberal view on the reality of the communist takeover in Russia

According to the historians Richard Pipes, Robert Conquest and Leonard Shapiro, the communist takeover of Russia was not just an event confined to a few days in October, but was a process stretching over several years. It began when Bolshevik revolutionaries seized control of the capital in October 1917, and then set about abolishing all the apparatus of democracy. Making false promises about delivering 'Peace, Bread and Land' to the peasants, the communists secretly hoped for a world revolution, and the nationalisation of land. When opponents started to be arrested and shot, and the elected assembly (of which the communists only won a quarter of the seats) was abolished at gunpoint, a civil war broke out. Millions died in the fighting, and Bolshevik economic policies (requisitioning to feed the army and the cities called War Communism) caused a famine in which millions more perished. An attempt by the sailors of Kronstadt to reduce Bolshevik authoritarianism was brutally suppressed in 1921 and the secret police carried out a reign of terror. Only by tightening the reigns of power could the Bolsheviks maintain their authority and this was to have disastrous consequences. There was a direct line between Lenin's takeover and the brutal regime of Stalin.

The libertarians and revisionists disagree on the role of Lenin and the people

The libertarians were eager to stress the leading role played by the people themselves in the Revolution. They wanted to show that the Russians had not just been the instruments of Lenin, and how they had, on several occasions, actually dictated events to the Bolsheviks. Stephen Smith examined the political influence of the factory workers in Petrograd and Sheila Fitzpatrick claimed that 'the people' had created the circumstances in which Lenin could act. The people had formed *Soviets* and made decisions ahead of the Bolsheviks. However, the fact remains that the Bolsheviks did assert themselves in the face of some opposition and indifference from the people. The voice of the majority, expressed in the election results, was silenced by the machine guns of the Red Guard and it was Lenin, albeit seeking approval at first, who made decisions that shaped the fortunes of millions of people. The revisionists and most recent historians, such as Robert Service and Chris Read, return to the idea that Lenin, whilst not fully in control of events or even of his party, was still important in 1917. Without him there would have been no October 'Revolution', and equally, without him, there may not have been the insistence of a disciplined, centralised, one-party state.

Tutorial

Progress questions

1. Why did the Soviet historians 'rewrite' the history of the October Revolution?
2. What evidence is there to support the libertarian idea that Lenin was not really in control of events in October 1917–January 1918?

3. How did the Bolsheviks deal with the lack of popular support and their opponents?
4. Comment on the 'inevitability' of the October Revolution.

Seminar discussion
'Lenin had no choice but to maintain his position through political terror.' Do you agree?

Practical assignment
1. Read the following narrative passage:

> 'After meeting for 12 hours (on the 18th January 1918), the Constituent Assembly was destined never to meet again. Lenin had decided in advance that the Assembly would be tested. If it endorsed the Bolsheviks' 'Declaration of Rights of the Toiling and Exploited Peoples' which stated that 'the Constituent Assembly unreservedly rallies to the policy of the Soviet authorities and feels that it would be quite wrong, even technically, to set itself up in opposition to...that power' (i.e. if it supported Soviet power) then it could be allowed to proceed. The Assembly rejected the Bolshevik motion (by 237 votes to 138) but did not put forward an alternative form of government to the Soviets.
>
> In the early hours of the morning of 19 January the Bolsheviks walked out, followed an hour later by the Left SRs. Lenin had already decided to abolish the Assembly and passed a motion declaring the Assembly dissolved on the same day.'

Now rewrite the paragraph in an analytical way, inserting evidence and any historical schools of thought you think are relevant. Add a conclusion, based on the context of the source.

2. The following descriptive paragraph is based on an extract by Chernov (the former Provisional Government's agriculture minister) on the fate of the Constituent Assembly.

> 'When we, the newly elected members of the Constituent Assembly, entered the Tauride Palace, the seat of the Assembly at Petrograd on 18 January 1918, we found that the corridors were full of armed guards. At first they did not address us directly, and only exchanged casual observations to the effect that – 'This guy should get a bayonet between his ribs' or 'It wouldn't be bad to put some lead into this one.'
>
> I delivered my inauguration address making vigorous efforts to keep self-control. Every sentence of my speech was met with outcries, some ironical, others spiteful, often buttressed by the brandishing of guns. I finished my

speech amidst a crossfire of interruptions and cries.

It was now the turn of the Bolshevik speakers. During their delivery our sector was a model of restraint and self-discipline. We maintained a cold, dignified silence. The Bolshevik speeches as usual were shrill, clamorous, provocative and rude, but they could not break the icy silence. Lenin, in the government box, demonstrated his contempt for the Assembly by lounging in his chair and putting on the air of a man who was bored to death.

When it appeared that we refused to vote the Soviet 'platform', without discussion the Bolsheviks walked out of the sitting in a body. I felt sure we would be arrested. But it was of utmost importance for us to have a chance to say the last word. I declared that the next point on the agenda was the land reform. At this moment somebody pulled at my sleeve. I proceeded to read the main paragraphs of the Land Bill, which our party had prepared long ago. But time was running short. Reports and debates had to be omitted. Upon my proposal the Assembly voted six basic points of the bill. It provided that all land was to be turned into common property, with every tiller possessing equal rights to use it. Amidst incessant shouts: 'That's enough!', 'Stop it now!', 'Clear the hall!' the other points of the bill were voted.

On the dawn of a foggy and murky morning I declared recess until noon. At noon several members of the Assembly were sent on reconnaissance. They reported that the door of the Tauride Palace was sealed and guarded by a patrol with machine guns. Thus ended Russia's first and last democratic parliament.'

V. Chernov, 'Russia's One Day Parliament',
The New Leader (31 January 1948)

1. Using the description above, give the Marxist interpretation of this event in one paragraph.
2. In a second paragraph, give an analytical view by a liberal historian.
3. Finally, drawing on the revisionist view, give a critical evaluation of the passage in a third paragraph.

Study tips

1. The best way to tackle this topic is to draw up a list of events first. Then, along each event, try to list all the factors that caused the events or the consequences of them – but keep this brief. Finally, add the interpretation by each 'school of thought'.
2. Keep in mind Lenin's motives. At each stage Lenin would have had an ideological 'blueprint' in his mind, but he was often forced to make adjustments by the force of events or for reasons of political expediency.

7

The Russian Civil War

One-minute summary – The Civil War had a profound impact on the shape of Russian communism that followed. The centralisation that Lenin preferred was used to reimpose discipline in the workplace and in the armed forces. Conscription and requisitioning (which is dealt with in the next chapter) were enforced with brutality. The reason for this was that the Bolsheviks were encircled and, in 1919, under pressure from armies on all points of the compass. However, despite several setbacks, the Bolsheviks managed to survive the Civil War. Whether this can be put down to the achievements of the Bolsheviks, or the errors of their enemies, is open to debate.

In this chapter you will learn:

► the course of the civil war
► the reasons for the Bolshevik victory
► the effects of the Civil War.

The course of the Civil War

The outbreak of the Civil War was caused by the Bolshevik dictatorship

The Bolshevik takeover in October had produced vocal opposition and some local resistance. Several people were killed in the weeks after the Revolution, but the establishment of a one-party dictatorship by Lenin, and the dissolution of the Constituent Assembly, convinced many Russians that the Bolsheviks could only be resisted by force. Lenin authorised the formation of the Red Army in January 1918, led by Trotsky. Anti-Red forces were nick-named 'Whites', but they were in no way united. Military commanders appointed themselves warlords, and factions across the political spectrum formed their own resistance groups. In the east, a group of Czech soldiers who had fought for Russia, augmented by Czech prisoners of war (from the Austro-Hungarian Imperial Army), had arranged to make their way to the West via the Trans-Siberian Railway. When local Bolshevik organisations tried to disarm the Czechs, fighting broke out. The Czechs formed themselves into a Czech Legion and battled it out for control of the railway, taking over vast stretches of territory. This fighting was the signal for other groups to take up arms against the Bolsheviks.

The Bolsheviks were surrounded

Generals Yudenich and Kornilov (who had escaped from prison) organised their own armies, the former in the north (Estonia) and the latter in the south (on the

River Don). The SRs declared their own government (having technically won the election) at Samara, called the Komuch. To the East, Admiral Kolchak declared himself 'Supreme Ruler of Russia' and head of the Omsk Government and he linked up with the Czech Legion. In the far south, along the Dnieper River, Makhno created an insurgent army of peasants who opposed centralised authority. The Ukraine, the Baltic States and Poland all formed national armies known as 'Greens'. Thus the Bolsheviks were encircled. To make matters worse, Britain sent troops to Murmansk in March 1918 (later Americans joined them while the French landed in Odessa and the Japanese took territory in the Far East). In June 1918, perhaps terrified by the prospect that he might provide the one unifying feature of the country, the Bolsheviks executed Tsar Nicholas II alongside his family at Ekaterinburg.

The fighting in the south

In the south, the Whites numbered 150,000 with a large contingent of the reknowned Don Cossacks. In the summer of 1918 they crossed the Don and laid siege to Tsaritsyn on the Volga. The commander of the Tsaritsyn garrison was Joseph Stalin and his orders were to hold the city at all costs. This was because the city kept apart the southern and eastern White armies and was the route through which vital grain supplies (requisitioned from peasants) could reach the cities of the north. The city was held and provided a brilliant propaganda coup for the Bolsheviks. As the years went by, and particularly when Stalin came to power, the defence of Stalingrad (it was renamed in his honour) was elevated to a heroic status. When Kornilov and his ally General Alekseev died in December 1918, General Denikin took over the 'Southern Volunteer Army' and he launched a second offensive in the summer of 1919. He captured Tsaritsyn (a point not mentioned in Soviet histories), Kharkov, Orel and came to within 320kms of Moscow, but was thrown back by a counter-attack by Trotsky and his reserves in November. Once the White Army was on the run, Trotsky pursued it until it virtually disintegrated. Denikin was replaced in 1920 by General Wrangel and he organised resistance from the Crimea. His force too was eventually defeated in November 1920.

The fighting in the east

Kolchak commanded an army of 140,000 and by June 1919, Kolchak's forces had crossed the Urals, taken Kazan and Samara, and were making their way towards Moscow. However, the Red Army counter-attacked just as SRs staged revolts against Kolchak's right-wing rule. His Czech allies also lacked any enthusiasm for the taking of Moscow. In the autumn, Kolchak was in retreat. In January 1919, he was captured, and executed a month later. The Czech Legion continued fighting, but after the declaration of Czech independence in October 1918 and the end of the war against Austria and Germany, the Legion broke up.

The fighting in the north

General Yudenich's army was only 15,000 strong but it reached the outskirts of Petrograd in October 1919. It was overwhelmed by greater numbers of Bolsheviks in November. The British forces that had arrived in March were deployed to reopen the war in the east against Germany (and thus divide the German effort), but Germany was defeated in November 1918. The British troops were ostensibly there to combat Bolshevism and support the Whites on the Arctic coast, but they were soon disillusioned by the corruption of White troops and were unenthusiastic about fighting yet another war. The French effort was also short lived; warship crews who were sent to protect French financial interests mutinied in the Black Sea. The Japanese seized territory in the Far East but had no interest in fighting the Bolshevik government. In central Asia, the British were eager to prevent Bolshevik propaganda spreading to India, their imperial dominion.

The Green Army of Nestor Makhno was a severe challenge to the Bolsheviks

Makhno's guerrilla armies were a sterner challenge for the Bolsheviks as they had already perfected their hit and run tactics against the Whites. Strongly supported by Ukrainian peasants, Makhno encouraged the formation of independent peasant communes (not unlike the traditional *Mirs*). The Bolsheviks, who claimed to represent the people, were actually trying to centralise control whereas Makhno was devolving authority in a more genuine communist way. The Bolsheviks therefore changed tactics. They enlisted Makhno as an ally during the latter stages of the civil war. However, as soon as the war was over, they crushed his peasant movement and Makhno was forced to take refuge in Romania.

Poland prevented 'world revolution'

Europe was probably saved from the worse excesses of Bolshevism by the efforts of the Polish. In 1919, they engaged Red forces in Western Russia, hoping to restore lands taken by the Russians over hundreds of years and in May 1920 they scored a major victory by taking Kiev. However, the Bolsheviks, who had now defeated most of their enemies, played on Russian nationalist sentiment (instead of their principle of international socialism) to repel the old enemy. Tukhachevsky, the commander of the Red Army in the region, drove the Poles back to Warsaw, meting out harsh punishments or executing his own men to motivate them. Lenin was encouraged by this success and, with communist uprisings in Berlin and other German cities, it seemed as if the moment of world revolution had arrived. Lenin and Trotsky envisaged rolling their army across Europe, enlisting proletarians on the way. Yet poor organisation and supply arrangements meant that the Poles, who had roused themselves to make one final defiant counter-attack, beat the Red Army. In Germany too, there was widespread hostility to the communists, especially since news of Bolshevik atrocities had been broadcast in the media. Fearing that the Poles might now march back into Russia, the Bolsheviks quickly concluded a peace treaty and accepted a new border line (called the Curzon Line) under the terms of the Treaty of Riga in 1921.

The reasons for the Bolshevik victory

Central position

The Bolsheviks transferred their capital to Moscow, the centre of the rail network, so that they could move troops from one front to another. Although they were surrounded, this was an advantage. White attacks were unco-ordinated and piecemeal. It was easier for the Bolsheviks to transfer troops along railway lines to deal with each threat in turn. In this way, they were able to utilise their smaller numbers to better effect. In addition, all the armaments works in Russia were in the industrial areas under Bolshevik control. Dense populations in central Russia also meant there was no shortage of manpower once the Bolsheviks began to conscript men (May 1918). Telegraph lines also radiated from the centre of Russia so communication was far easier than for the Whites who had no way of keeping in contact with each other.

Organisation and discipline

The Bolsheviks had a single chain of command and imposed strict discipline. In 1918 Trotsky ordered that: 'Every scoundrel who incites anyone to retreat, to desert, or not to fulfil a military order, will be shot. Every soldier who voluntarily deserts his post will be shot. Every soldier who throws away his rifle or sells part of his equipment will be shot.' This discipline was in stark contrast to the Soviet Order No.1 of March 1917, and it was ruthlessly exercised. The Whites were hopelessly divided, and held different beliefs or war aims. National minorities tended to fight for their own interests and there was no common purpose. White generals did not trust each other and no one trusted Kolchak's ambitions.

Trotsky's leadership

Trotsky's record in the Civil War has become an area of historical controversy. Bolshevik propaganda in the 1920s elevated his achievement, but in the 1930s, Stalin expunged Trotsky from any credit at all. Trotsky, like many commanders made some mistakes and suffered setbacks, but he also achieved a great deal. He turned the Red Army from an ill-disciplined 'flabby and panicky mass' into a force to be reckoned with, although it was not so perfect that it could defeat the Poles in 1920–21. Trotsky did lead by example, gave inspiring speeches to his men, and rushed reserves to the points of greatest danger. He also exercised great brutality. Peasant conscripts in the Red Army (the majority by the end of the war) knew that if they tried to retreat they would be machine gunned by their own side. The White officers were less brutal but just as callous. They were indifferent to the conditions of their troops and treated soldiers with contempt. Consequently desertion was rife. Corruption was an epidemic. Military equipment was stolen and sold on the black market; some of it even ended up in Red Army hands.

Support for the Reds was not always voluntary

The peasants supported neither side in the Civil War with any enthusiasm and served their own interests. Many warmed to the promises made by Lenin that land would go to the peasants, whereas the Whites promised only to restore land to their former owners. Peasant soldiers made up the bulk of troops on both sides and deserted whenever they could. In addition, national minorities refused to co-operate with the Whites who wanted a restoration of the pre-revolutionary imperial borders. Lenin accepted the secession of the minorities with reluctance (it may have been a short-term calculation to divide his enemies). In the cities, the Reds were able to provide some food and fuel and the urban populations saw that the Bolsheviks, however unfair their political arrangements, were prioritising what they needed. The fact that grain was being requisitioned from the countryside at gunpoint did not matter to the starving urban populations. Hunger was also a great motivating factor for former Tsarist officers. The promise of food and pay enticed them to join the Red Army and Trotsky encouraged this, despite criticism from the party members. He needed their expertise, but he held their families hostage to make sure of their 'loyalty'. Trotsky placated the party by appointing political commissars to supervise each military unit and report on its attitude; dissent was punishable by death. Soldiers were no longer permitted to elect their officers or to have committees. Ranks were reintroduced, saluting restored and different pay scales were arranged. Middle-class men were forced to join Labour Battalions to do manual work at the Front. The Red Army numbered three million in 1919 and five million in 1920, but four million had deserted the Red Army during its existence from 1918–21.

Bolshevik propaganda was more striking

The Bolsheviks made much of the fact that the Whites were receiving the support of foreign powers, even though the amount of assistance was very small. Soviet propaganda played on the idea that the Bolsheviks were offering the peasants their own land, and a new society for workers. The Whites made little use of propaganda, hoping for military success instead. What is not clear is how effective Bolshevik propaganda was. Despite all the draconian measures against deserters, men continued to abandon the Red Army, and there was still resentment about the Bolshevik monopoly of power (and the dismissive attitude towards the *Soviets*). The Bolsheviks denounced any criticism outside of the party as counter-revolutionary, which could result in severe punishments. People began to watch what they said, but many still voted with their feet and gave only half-hearted support to the Bolshevik cause.

Historians interpret the Civil War differently

Once again, Soviet historians later claimed that the Civil War was won because the Bolsheviks enjoyed the universal and overwhelming support of the working class. Liberal historians tended to focus on the reign of terror and fear that motivated people to back the Bolsheviks. Libertarians tended to see the people as victims of the Bolshevik government and the Civil War they unleashed on them.

They also draw attention to the betrayal of the principles of the original revolution of 1917. Revisionists would now see how narrowly the Bolsheviks won the Civil War. It was not an inevitable victory. Indeed, they also show how the harsh measures needed in the Civil War influenced the regime later.

The effects of the civil war

Atrocities and disease

A common feature of civil wars is the incidence of atrocities and the Russian conflict was no exception. Both sides committed acts of great barbarity. Villages that appeared to have shown loyalty to one side could be slaughtered, man, woman and child, if overrun by the other. Looting by troops could leave families without the means to survive, particularly in the sub-zero temperatures of a Russian winter. Kiev changed hands sixteen times, Cossack units changed sides and sometimes murdered their own officers. In the south, Cossacks raped and murdered 115,000 Ukranian Jews in their villages, accusing them of being Bolsheviks. Whites also killed miners who did not work hard enough and buried hundreds of them alive at Rostov. Reds nailed epaulettes to the shoulders of captured white officers. Suspects were routinely and summarily executed, as were their own troops who did not fight to the local commander's satisfaction. Disease also played its part. Typhus and typhoid killed half a million Russians during the Civil War period. The collapse of the country's infrastructure, the carriage of disease by roaming armies and the contamination of water supplies caused these deaths, but ultimately the responsibility for the carnage must lie with those who perpetuated war and revolution.

The truth about revolutions

Russia's catastrophes were a direct result of the civil war, itself a product of revolution. Revolutions throughout history have produced social anarchy, an upsurge of crime, civil war, and, as a means of bringing this process under control, dictatorships of great brutality. In each case, extremist ideologies have been used to justify the brutalities of a political minority. Against these harsh historical realities, it is hard to see why some continue to see revolutions as romantic and liberating episodes. The truth is that they result in untold suffering, misery and death.

An attempt to kill Lenin intensified the Red Terror

On 30 August 1918, the SR member, Fanya Kaplan, managed to shoot Lenin, hitting him in the neck. He survived, but it was a turning point in the way that Lenin was portrayed. Up until that point, few pictures of Lenin were produced and because of the risk of assassination, he rarely appeared on the streets. Although he was only wounded in 1918, the Bolshevik propagandists converted Lenin into a god-like figure, heroically prepared to risk his life for the revolution.

It also gave Lenin the excuse to unleash the Cheka, an organisation that built on the existing terror methods being exercised because of the Civil War. If Russians were already suffering, then it was about to get worse.

Tutorial

Progress questions
1. What were the weaknesses of the White forces?
2. How important were the foreign interventions in the Civil War?
3. What was the significance of Makhno's forces?
4. Why did the Civil War result in atrocities?

Seminar discussion
'Was it not the case that: the Reds did not win, the Whites lost?'. Discuss.

Practical assignment
Try to identify the political aspects of the Civil War as well as the military. One way to do this is to extract onto a table or diagram the political authorities engaged in the civil war, their beliefs and their fate. You should include: the Tsar, Lenin and the Bolsheviks, Admiral Kolchak, the SRs, the Allies and the Greens.

Study tips
1. The Civil War is a complex topic. A good way to get a grasp of the war is to make a sketch map of Russia and annotate around the edge of the map the forces and the significant dates/events.
2. Keep your notes brief and clear. A bullet point list of why the Reds won will be more effective than a full side of dense, handwritten notes.

8

The Economy and the Consolidation of Communism

One-minute summary – When the Bolsheviks concluded a hasty peace treaty with Germany at Brest Litovsk in March 1918, they lost 62 million people, 27% of farm land, 26% of railway lines and 74% of iron ore and coal reserves. Even after the Civil War, Finland, Poland and the Baltic States remained outside the Soviet Union. The Civil War itself worsened Russia's economic decline and it was years before Russia regained her pre-1914 strength. However, perhaps worst of all was the fact that Lenin's determination to run Russia along lines laid down in Marxist theory led to one of Russia's most devastating famines. Only when his most loyal supporters, the Kronstadt sailors, were driven to armed resistance and millions had died, did Lenin relent and permit a modicum of capitalism to return. The result was instant: the beginning of recovery. Nevertheless, the Bolsheviks still aimed to resume their policies of centralisation and state direction as soon as possible, and they tightened up on discipline both inside the party and in the general population. Lenin ordered harsh reprisals against any opposition. Stalin inherited this system.

In this chapter you will learn:

▶ why Lenin implemented War Communism
▶ the reasons for the switch to a New Economic Policy
▶ the effects of Lenin's policies.

War Communism

The Bolshevik economy was collapsing

When Lenin had seized power, he had been unable to coerce the people into the acceptance of communist doctrine and had to concentrate on accepting whatever demands were popular to build up support. Consequently, the peasants had taken over the land as private owners, and small committees of workers had taken over factories. The workers proved incapable of running the factories efficiently, and shortages of raw materials (caused by the Civil War) made the situation worse. As production fell, so the scarcity and price of goods increased. The value of the rouble collapsed and paper money became virtually worthless. Peasants saw no value in exchanging food for roubles and the fall in production meant there were few goods to buy anyway. As Ukraine, the granary of Russia, had been lost, there was a food shortage and the Petrograd ration fell to 50 grams per person per day.

By the spring of 1918 there were food riots in Bolshevik areas. Urban populations fled the cities, back into the countryside. Far from turning the Russian population into a class-conscious proletariat, Lenin's people were starving and returning to subsistence agriculture.

Lenin established war communism

Facing the onslaught of White armies, Lenin declared a new policy called 'war communism'. His priorities were to supply and equip the Red Army to win the Civil War, to feed the proletariat remaining in the cities, to keep the workers in the factories to maintain production. All these were essential if Lenin was to remain in power. The main features of the policy were the requisitioning of grain from the peasantry, the banning of private trade, the nationalisation of all industry, the introduction of rationing and an increase in labour discipline.

The requisitioning of grain from the peasants and state terror

Red Guards and Bolshevik activists were sent into the countryside to seize food supplies from the peasants. In May 1918, the Food Supplies Dictatorship formalised this policy across all occupied areas. The peasants resisted the forced seizures and began to lynch the squads sent to take their food. In one example, peasants decapitated twelve Red Army men and stuck their heads on poles as a warning. The Red Army responded with equal violence, as did the Cheka. Quotas were drawn up and fulfilled even if this left the peasants starving: in theory, the proletariat came first but the requisition squads behaved little better than bandits. Lenin's solution was to try to 'divide and rule'. He ordered that *Kulaks* (rich peasants) be hanged in public to terrorise others and he tried to foster a class resentment amongst poorer peasants. It failed. Lenin then ordered widespread arrests but the peasants retaliated by hiding grain and refused to plant for the next year's harvest. Wheat production collapsed. In fury and frustration, Lenin set up concentration camps and labour camps for all dissidents from urban and rural areas. It was clear that he intended to crush opposition by force.

Private trade was banned

In accordance with communist theory, all private exchange was abolished. However, the state trading authority was in chaos (as well as being corrupt) so a black market of secret private trade flourished. For many, this was the only way to stay alive.

The nationalisation of all industry

Also in accordance with Marxist theory, all industry was placed in the hands of the state which represented the people. Administration was handled by the *Vesenkha* (Supreme Council of National Economy) which were appointed 'specialists' to replace the workers' committees. In fact the 'specialists' were really the former managers brought back to run their old firms. The workers' committees had been a hopeless experiment: they had given themselves huge pay rises, stolen factory parts for private sale and made a loss. Some workers realised that without central control and nationalisation the factories would close and they would lose their jobs, and thus their only income for survival. This aspect of communism was concealed from the outside world, and left-wing movements continued to advocate nationalisation and workers' control, unaware of the damage it had caused to the Russian economy.

The introduction of rationing and an increase in labour discipline

The proletariat and the Red Army were given a preference in the distribution of rations. A smaller ration was given to civil servants and professionals, whilst the bourgeoisie were given a starvation ration. This system was designed to encourage loyalty to the regime, but there was also a tightening of discipline. Lateness and absenteeism were punished with fines. Internal passports were issued to prevent people leaving the cities. Piece rate was reintroduced, along with bonuses and extra rations for evidence of work. Still there was anger at the starvation levels in the cities and the lack of freedoms promised by the revolution. In Petrograd, there were demands for the recalling of the Constituent Assembly, for a free press and the abolition of one-party dictatorship. One slogan on a wall read: 'Down with Lenin and horsemeat! Give us the Tsar and pork!'

The Terror became the hallmark of communist rule

The Cheka responded to the increase of dissent with more brutality. Executions became the normal punishment and many were shot without any form of trial. The 'official' figure was 13,000 but conservative estimates put the figure nearer 300,000. Some talked of exterminating the middle class and all counter-revolutionaries, without defining exactly who these people were. Many social groups were targeted. Workers and peasants, former noblemen, prostitutes, judges, businessmen, and even children (accused of 'bourgeois provocation') were imprisoned. Priests were forced to renounce their faith with a gun against their head, and many were martyred for their refusal to do so. In some cases, priests were stripped naked in front of their villages' congregations and ordered to tell the peasants they had lied to them. The Cheka's headquarters, the Lubianka in Moscow, soon became notorious for its torture and executions. Felix Dzerzhinsky, its fanatical chief, remarked: 'The Cheka does not judge – it strikes'. However, the Terror was only loosely linked to the economic crisis. Lenin had always believed that during the 'Dictatorship of the Proletariat' he would have to wage war on class enemies. The Terror was a useful tool for this, but it also ensured compliance and discipline amongst the rest of the population. It was a means of control. Robert Service argues that Lenin gave vent to his passionate anger once in power. He seemed to be consumed by a desire for 'revenge'.

War Communism continued after the Civil War

After the Civil War was over, the need for War Communism seemed to be over, but its effect of giving the Bolsheviks control of the workforce and its closeness to communist economic principles (a centrally directed or command economy), made Lenin loathe to give it up. Trotsky even advocated the 'militarisation of labour'; that is, the transfer of Red Army soldiers to the farms and factories whilst maintaining the military discipline he had introduced. Despite the image, the Bolshevik party was not as organised or as well disciplined as it seemed. Bolshevik party members participated in the black market just like everyone else. Local Bolshevik party leaders set themselves up as mafia bosses. The 5,000 leading Bolsheviks in Moscow lived in hotels, attended by bodyguards, and prostitutes, many of them young women from former 'bourgeois families' who would sell themselves for a few pieces of bread or some soup. Champagne and caviar were served by the 'comrade waiters', and bribes of food, fuel, tobacco and alcohol were common. Many Russians resented the fact that party members' wives lorded it over others, bedecked with looted jewellery.

The crisis of 1921

By 1921, the Russian economy was in crisis. The transport system was falling apart and production was falling. In the cities, hungry people stalked the streets in search of food. In the countryside, there was famine. Millions died, their skeletal bodies gradually exhausted until they collapsed. The requisitioning had done its worst and the Bolshevik policy coincided that year with a drought in the south. In the remoter parts of the country, some turned to cannibalism. In the days before the complete censorship of the media had been enforced, some images have survived of this terrible event. For all the abuses of Tsarism, there had never been a disaster like this before the communists, and the most criminal thing about it was that it was perpetrated by Stalin on an even greater scale all over again in the 1930s. The peasants did not all die without some show of resistance. When the requisitioning squads arrived with new and unbelievably high quotas in 1921, there were revolts. In the Tambov region, for example, Alexander Antonov led a guerrilla force against the Red Army. The winter of 1920–21 had been particularly severe and so the bread ration was cut by one third in several cities. Bread riots broke out and the Cheka had to open fire. Red Army troops refused to do so and the party spokesmen were shouted down at meetings. There was widespread anger at the way that new factory regulations meant that men could be shot for failing to meet targets. There were demands for the *Soviets* to be purged of all communists. Martial law was declared in Moscow and Petrograd by the authorities. It seemed that February 1917 was about to be repeated but this time Lenin was to be toppled.

The Kronstadt Revolt

In March, the Kronstadt sailors, the heroes of the Bolshevik coup in 1917, rose up in rebellion against the communists. They demanded free speech, new elections and secret ballots, the liberation of all political prisoners, the abolition of a one-party dictatorship and the freedom of the peasants to farm unmolested by the state. Lenin reacted swiftly. Tukhachevsky, now a Marshal, was directed by Lenin and Trotsky to attack Kronstadt naval base. A bitter struggle took place across the ice and the sailors were shown no quarter as they were overrun. There were thousands of casualties. The ringleaders who were captured alive were executed. The survivors were sent to a labour camp at Solovetsky. The rising had indicated just how unpopular the Bolsheviks had become. Even within their own party a group set itself up called the Workers' Opposition. They called for an end to the militaristic conditions in the factories and opposed the state control of the trade unions that was being proposed by Trotsky. Lenin realised that if they did not alter their polices, the Bolsheviks would not survive in power. Although Trotsky believed that it was more discipline that was needed, not less, Lenin knew that this would split the party. More than anything else, this incident indicated that Marxist-Leninism did not represent the interests of the people, and that communism was a dictatorship hiding behind the façade of a 'people's government'.

The escalation of repression continued after 1921

Lenin continued to enforce strict discipline against the Russian people, and the rising at Kronstadt provided a perfect excuse to act against his enemies. Five thousand Mensheviks and SRs were arrested and imprisoned (even though they had become more popular during the unrest of 1921). They were accused of 'counter-revolutionary activities', which included encouraging strikes and demonstrations against Bolshevik rule. The first show trials were introduced. SRs were forced to 'confess' to plots against Lenin or collaboration with Whites in the Civil War (even when some of them had actually been in prison at the time). Eleven were executed. Red Army units poured into areas of peasant unrest, burning villages and executing ringleaders. Propaganda was used to extol the virtue of co-operating with the regime and the New Economic Policy (NEP) (see below). Angry about a revival of support for the church, the Bolsheviks established the 'Union of the Militant Godless' organisation in 1921. Under its authority, troops and party men stripped churches of their valuables and persecuted the clergy. The death penalty was passed against priests. Censorship was imposed more thoroughly. In 1922, many writers and scholars were exiled. Books, poems, and other literature had to be submitted to the Main Administration for Affairs of Literature and Publishing Houses for 'approval'. That same year, the Cheka was renamed the GPU. It continued to harass the citizens of Russia, particularly 'Nepmen' (see below) whom they regarded as class enemies. Arbitrary arrests and murders also continued.

The New Economic Policy

The Bolsheviks had become an unpopular group of rulers, as the resistance in the countryside and at Kronstadt had proved. To hold on to power, Lenin was prepared to make some changes. However, in the Politburo Bukharin stated: 'We are making economic concessions to avoid political concessions'. Some Bolsheviks regarded the change to a New Economic Policy, which involved private enterprise, as a 'betrayal of Marxist principles', but the criticism seemed unjustified when even the Bolsheviks' most loyal supporters rebelled in the Kronstadt Revolt. However, all agreed that NEP was a temporary policy. There were four main elements to NEP:

▶ *Grain requisitions were abolished.* Demands for all the peasants' grain were replaced by a tax in kind, that is a portion of their food (far less than the squads had taken), and any surplus could be sold for profit on the open market. This free enterprise was in direct contradiction of Marxist principles.

▶ *Small businesses were permitted.* Small businesses were allowed to be developed by private owners and permitted to make a profit. This free enterprise was also in direct contradiction of Marxist principles. Lenin was in favour of the small workshops that made boots, nails and clothes, as these were the things peasants would purchase and exchange their food for.

▶ *The ban on private trading was lifted.* When private trade was permitted again, a flow of food into the towns and cities resumed almost instantly. Small shops reopened. Rationing was ended and Russians had to budget for food from their income. Private entrepreneurs soon emerged and there was now an incentive to work harder, to earn more and therefore to eat well. This was capitalism.

▶ *State control of industry maintained centralisation.* The party kept control of industries such as coal, steel, oil, public transport and banking. However, it permitted industries to form Trusts, which could decide on wages and costs of production. This was a limited return to private ownership, whilst retaining a supervisory role. This prevented the return of finance capital ventures that were so important to the countries of Western Europe. Wall Street and the City of London's Stock Market were capable of generating huge surpluses of finance that could be reinvested and used to develop the country. Therefore, in Russia, capitalism was flourishing at grass roots level but it was being stifled at the higher level.

The effects of Lenin's economic policies

NEP was a great success. Food poured back into the cities, and cafés reopened. There was a general normalisation of the economy. Grain production increased by 23% from 1920–23. In the same period, factory production grew by 200%, as demand mushroomed and wealth returned. Heavy industry recovered more slowly, but the reintroduction of free capitalism was certainly helping. Those that purchased peasants' produce and transported it for sale in the cities, and then returned the city goods were nick-named 'Nepmen'. They made enormous profits, which they used to bribe reluctant party officials. They were more ruthless than the old bourgeoisie and less inhibited by the social codes of the old days. They wanted to make money and enjoy the profits. Crime and prostitution increased. Property speculation returned.

The 'scissors crisis' forced further liberalisation of the economy

The volume of food flowing into the cities became a flood by 1923, lowering the value of it and therefore its price. At the same time, industrial goods were still hard to come by and the price increased. Trotsky called this the 'scissors crisis' because of the appearance of the two price curves on a graph. To solve the crisis, the Bolshevik government brought an end to the 'tax in kind' system and compelled peasants to pay tax in cash. They also lowered the price of industrial goods by intervention.

Private enterprise was a success but Lenin was insincere

The NEP delighted the peasants. They made profits from the sale of produce and made additional money from sales to Nepmen. They could also farm their land as they liked and live from the surpluses they produced. Government interference was less than at any time since 1917. The whole NEP policy demonstrated just how little the Bolsheviks really understood about running an economy, which was ironic since Marxism claimed to be a doctrine based on economics. Bolshevik insistence on a centrally directed, or 'command, economy had led to famine and millions of deaths. Their mismanagement had fomented a boiling resentment in 1921, and they averted a full-scale revolution only by the abandonment of their principles and the adoption of NEP. Yet Lenin was arrogant enough to believe that as soon as the country had recovered, he would return to the doctrinaire precepts of Marxism. He intended to abolish all private ownership as soon as was feasible. In this sense, the Bolsheviks seemed to be eager to make war on their own people, politically, militarily or economically. The centralisation of the state went on, and the violence of the secret police did not abate.

Tutorial

Progress questions

1. To what extent was Lenin a 'Red Tsar' by inclination?
2. 'By the end [of his life], there was little to show for the great communist utopia Lenin had set out to build'. Do you agree?
3. 'Inconsistent plans that ended in unmitigated disaster.' How valid is this verdict on Lenin's economic policies?

4. 'Butcher, tyrant, and deceiver' or 'pioneer, champion of the oppressed and martyr'. Which of these verdicts best fits Lenin as leader of Russia and the Bolshevik party, 1918–21?

Seminar discussion
1. 'Inefficient and inept, rather than malicious in intent'. Do you agree with this verdict on Lenin's economic policies?
2. Does Lenin appear to be a more or less important figure in shaping events between 1918 and 1921?

Practical assignment
Read the following passage, known as the *Hanging Order*:

'11 August 1918
Send to Penza To Comrades Kuraev, Bosh, Minkin and other Penza communists:

Comrades! The revolt by the five kulak volost's must be suppressed without mercy. The interest of the entire revolution demands this, because we have now before us our final decisive battle "with the kulaks." We need to set an example.

1. You need to hang (hang without fail, so that the public sees) at least 100 notorious kulaks, the rich, and the bloodsuckers.
2. Publish their names.
3. Take away all of their grain.
4. Execute the hostages - in accordance with yesterday's telegram.

This needs to be accomplished in such a way, that people for hundreds of miles around will see, tremble, know and scream out: let's choke and strangle those blood-sucking kulaks.
Telegraph us acknowledging receipt and execution of this.
Yours, *Lenin*
P.S. Use your toughest people for this.'

[Translator's comments: Lenin uses the derogative term *kulach'e* in reference to the class of prosperous peasants. A *volost'* was a territorial/administrative unit consisting of a few villages and surrounding land.]

1. Why was this order sent, and what was its purpose?
2. How might Liberal and Libertarian historians have used this source? (Note that Marxist historians concealed this document.).

Study tips

1. It is a good idea to review how the various schools of thought would interpret the events in the period 1918–21.
2. Note how vital Kronstadt was in changing Lenin's policies. Lenin himself said that it had 'lit up reality'.
3. Be aware of how political controls continued to be tightened even when the economy was liberalised. This suggests that political power was Lenin's priority.

9

The Lenin Dictatorship and the Rise of Stalin

One-minute summary – Was Lenin a Red Tsar? Did his government lead directly to the horrors of Stalinism? These questions have divided historians and have often been discussed through intensely ideological perspectives. Broadly, Western historians saw Stalin's regime as the logical outcome of Lenin's communist coup and centralising government. Communism was the problem, but the personality of Stalin made this oppressive political system excessively brutal. Left-wing historians tried to draw a distinction between Lenin, a benign, pioneering figure and Stalin, a violent man who turned the revolution from its true path into a dictatorship. Yuri Afanasyev called Stalin's regime 'unnatural, illegal and [one which] contradicted the ideas, traditions and history of socialism'. The Soviet Union, and particularly Khrushchev in the so-called Secret Speech, used the differences between Lenin and Stalin to exonerate the ideology of communism itself, but there was little attempt to dismantle the government apparatus that Lenin and Stalin had built up. When Gorbachev began the process of restructuring (*perestroika*) in the late 1980s, to bring in more democracy and openness (*glasnost*), the centralised system fell apart and communism was rejected by the people. It suggests that Stalin's method of rule was the only one that could ensure communism would survive. Once the party relaxed its grip, the people would turn away from the rigid demands and half-truths of the left.

In this chapter you will learn:

▶ was Lenin really a 'Red Tsar'?
▶ how Stalin made use of the Lenin cult and secured power
▶ how Stalin dealt with his opposition
▶ the definition of Stalinism.

Was Lenin really a 'Red Tsar'?

Lenin's ideas were hardly democratic

Lenin's political ideas even before the revolution exhibit all the tendencies of an extremist: he believed that, because Russia did not have a well-developed proletariat and because revolutionaries had been shot down by the forces of order in the past (like the Paris Commune, 1871, or the 1848 revolutions in Europe), success depended on a highly disciplined revolutionary elite. They would not participate in democratic politics but would seize power by force, using violence against anyone who stood in their way. Lenin saw democracy as a serving a purpose, to win over the proletariat, but it was to be a temporary measure on the road to full power. This was in stark contrast to all other revolutionary parties or groups who felt that the appeal should be as broad as possible. Lenin had no time for the peasantry, clearly feeling (as Marx had done later in life, that they were a counter-revolutionary and conservative force who filled the ranks of the army of the state). Like the old Tsars, Lenin assumed absolute power.

Lenin created a centralised state

Lenin also picked up on Marx's prediction that there would need to be a period immediately after the revolution called the Dictatorship of the Proletariat. Marx felt that this period of force would be needed to create a classless society, but he wasn't any more specific than that. Lenin took it to mean the ruthless imposition of the 'socialist order'. Private property would be abolished and those that opposed them (such as the 'former people') would be re-educated, or shot. Lenin established a secret police that was known for its terror and brutality. If Lenin had really intended there to be a moderate, democratic result to his assumption of power, he made no attempt to dismantle the highly centralised state he had created. He was only concerned by the rise of bureaucracy, and not by the power his party wielded. Again, Lenin's brand of government was not unlike the old Tsarist state.

Lenin made several mistakes and was the victim of events

He was not in Russia when the revolution occurred (February 1917) and the proletariat were not the only revolutionary force in Russia. The peasants and the peasant-soldiers of the army were perhaps the primary revolutionaries because of the conditions thrown up by the war. By contrast, the revolutionary parties, including the Bolsheviks, failed to take power in February. The *Duma* deputies did and the provisional government initially enjoyed wide support. The Bolsheviks were initially unable to penetrate the *Soviets* until they abandoned their hostility to private ownership (that is, when they altered the slogan 'Peace, Bread and Land'). Lenin only made any progress when the provisional government had failed to provide what people wanted. Even so, Lenin's attempts to take over in July 1917 failed and he had to flee for his life and only seized power when support for the provisional government in Petrograd had evaporated. He erroneously assumed that power in Petrograd would give him power over Russia. Lenin's coup provoked Russia's bloodiest civil war which was only narrowly won. His war communism of 1918 (a slavish following of the communist ideas of common ownership) was a disaster and almost provoked a revolution against him. His dictatorship and mismanagement provoked a rebellion amongst his staunchest supporters in 1921: the sailors of Kronstadt. Lenin's solution was to have them all shot and his successors followed his precedent of rewriting history to suit the new ideological interpretation. Finally, he failed to safeguard Russia against ruthless or ambitious successors like Trotsky and Stalin. These points suggest Lenin was often as unsuccessful as the last Tsar, blundering through decisions and using force to produce the desired result.

Lenin achieved a remarkable change in Russia

Lenin was a determined leader who emerged against all the odds to become a revered icon in Russia for 70 years in a way that the Tsars had been exalted (they embalmed him, built statues, renamed streets and even a city after him). He swept away democracy (not Tsarism, that had already gone) and imposed a classless society. All property and industry was placed in the hands of the state. These measures were designed to remove inequalities of wealth and social injustice. Promotion would be due, not to birth and wealth, but to dedication to the people. Individualism and selfish behaviour was considered a crime against the people; everything had to be shared (including the peasants' food). Education was made a priority. Without advanced technology, the Russians fell back on their only other resource: manpower. The Civil War undoubtedly delayed Russia's reconstruction, but Lenin made the first steps and, with Trotsky, was something of an inspiration. Stalin felt that Russia's survival depended on modernisation, so he continued Russia's development at a ruthless pace, invoking Lenin's name to legitimise his actions. Lenin's enthusiasm inspired many followers who were determined to make communism a success and they were prepared to make huge sacrifices for this mission. In this respect, Lenin also commanded the respect and following that had formally been accorded to the Tsars.

Lenin was uncomfortable with idolisation

Lenin had not set out to become a Tsar. He deplored the Lenin cult that had sprung up after the assassination attempt of 1921 and forbade any statues of himself being erected. He genuinely believed in Marxist doctrine and was trying to implement this blueprint for the greater, long-term good, and certainly not for himself. He remained in humble, middle-class accommodation (with a summer *dacha*) after securing power, rather than residing in any of the former Tsarist palaces. The worship of Lenin was a device exploited by Stalin, who understood the desire amongst less educated people for a personality to look up to. It would be fair to say that Lenin had all the powers of a Tsar, indeed more than they had had, but he remained wedded to Marxism. Whether he would have begun to dismantle the centralised state had he lived longer is a matter of great debate. Even if he intended to do so eventually, he gave no indication that the party's power would be diluted and he was still advocating greater centralisation in his last active years. Lenin did not see himself as a Tsar and he would have denied that what his party was doing was Tsarism. The greatest irony is, that in trying to overturn the inequalities and excesses of Tsarist and capitalist Russia, Lenin created a regime that was just as unfair, brutal and intolerant. It is Lenin who must shoulder that historical responsibility.

Lenin's Political Testament was critical of his colleagues

Lenin suffered a stroke in 1921 and then several more until his death in 1924. The year before his death he had lost the power of speech. When he was relieved of the task of running the party in 1922, he dedicated himself to reviewing the changes

Similarities	Differences
One Party State Both leaders banned other parties and maintained a dictatorship of one party. **Terror** Both used terror to further their ambitions, crush opponents and both set up secret police forces that answered only to the highest echelons of the Party, if not themselves. **Centralisation** Both men carried out a policy of concentrating power into their hands as the most efficient way of running the country. **Distanced from the people** Both men became detached from the realities of people's lives. Both were convinced that they knew the right path to follow and coerced others into following it. In the 1920s, Lenin grew critical of the uncultured nature of the proletariat. **Abolition of Party democracy** Stalin continued a process Lenin had begun: the removal of dissenting voices within the Party and in the country. Both were in favour of purging the Party of those elements that did not adhere with loyalty to the Party line as they dictated it. **Economy** Both believed strongly in centralised planning and state ownership.	**Cult of Personality** Lenin disliked the idea but Stalin fostered it. Lenin did, however, applaud the idea of propaganda and encouraged it. **Purges** Lenin may have wished to have a streamlined and disciplined Party, but he limited his terror to others. Stalin was content to terrorise his own supporters as much as any potential enemies. Stalin murdered on a huge scale, but Lenin's violence appeared to be more directed (if equally irrational and brutal). **World Revolution** Stalin abandoned the idea for 'socialism in one country'. **National minorities** Lenin appeared to tolerate different nationalities, as long as they accepted his will. Stalin seemed to have a pathological hatred of other nationalities, although this may just seem so because of the punishments he meted out to the people of the Soviet Union. **Leninism and Stalinism** Concepts have come to have different meanings. Stalinism is associated with totalitarianism, but Lenin's reputation, and therefore the concept of Leninism appears to be associated with revolutionary action.

Figure 4. Lenin and Stalin: A comparison.

taking place. He was critical of the growth of a party bureaucracy which seemed to be developing a life of its own. In March 1922, at the Eleventh Party Congress, Lenin asked: 'If we take that gigantic bureaucratic heap, we must ask: who is directing whom?... To tell the truth, they [the Communist Party] are not directing, they are being directed.' Nevertheless, Lenin was also critical of those who wanted more democracy in the party, led by a group called the Workers' Opposition. The group was outlawed and the party was purged of 'newcomers' (critics) in 1921. Lenin also drew up a Political Testament on 25 December 1922. In it, it warned that Trotsky, perhaps the favourite to be Lenin's successor, was given to a 'too far-reaching self confidence'. Stalin, he warned, 'has concentrated an enormous power in his hands' and added 'I am not sure that he always knows how to use that power with sufficient caution'. Lenin was referring to the Georgian Affair where Stalin had bullied and beaten local Bolsheviks into a hard line against Mensheviks and other opponents. He was reported to have said that the USSR should be governed from Moscow 'as the Tsars had done', a comment that earned from Lenin the sobriquet the 'Great Russian Chauvinist'. Lenin also predicted a split in the party between Trotsky and Stalin.

How Stalin made use of the Lenin cult and secured power

Stalin exploited Lenin's illness and death

Stalin placed his wife as Lenin's secretary and was provided with a stream of information about Lenin's views. When Stalin insulted Krupskaya on the telephone, Lenin added a postscript to his testament suggesting that Stalin be removed from the post of general secretary to the party. News of this reached Stalin but Lenin died before action was taken. Stalin moved swiftly to arrange the funeral and persuaded Trotsky, who was recuperating from an illness, not to attend. This damaged Trotsky's reputation later. Amidst a public outpouring of grief, Stalin orchestrated the funeral and made a speech about continuing Lenin's work. Whilst he was working to suppress Lenin's criticisms of him in the Testament, Stalin encouraged a Lenin cult. Posters and memorabilia were produced, and statues were erected. Lenin's brain was removed from his body and cut into 30,000 slices for scientific study – to discover his genius. At this stage, few believed that Stalin was suitable or likely to take power for himself.

Stalin was dismissed as unimportant by rivals

Stalin's real name was Joseph Dzhugashvili, the son of a devout Georgian family of peasant stock. Beaten as a child, Joseph developed a strong personal discipline and joined a Marxist group where he engaged in bank robberies and organised strikes. He was arrested and exiled several times to Siberia where he endured tough conditions, but he escaped and was in Petrograd soon after the February Revolution in 1917. He was made the editor of *Pravda* and occupied a seat on the executive committee of the Petrograd *Soviet*. However, he played no role in the events of October but was given the job of Commissar of Nationalities by Lenin in the new administration. In the crisis of the Civil War, Stalin was despatched to Tsaritsyn (later Stalingrad) to organise the defence and food supplies. He fell out with Trotsky over the defence of the region and they developed a personal animosity. Stalin was removed from his post because of frequent disobedience. In 1919, Stalin was given the job of Workers and Peasants Inspectorate (the *Rabkhrin*), a department which oversaw the work of the Civil Service and became a virtual police force, and Lenin also gave this grey and dull administrator command of the *Orgburo* (control of party organisation) since it was a task no one else wanted. He was correspondingly placed in the *Politburo* (the equivalent of a cabinet) before taking up the job of Party General Secretary. Sukhanov, who wrote his memoirs about the party leaders, described Stalin as a: 'grey blur which flickered obscurely and left no trace'.

Stalin and his opposition

Stalin used his positions to achieve power

All eyes were focussed on Trotsky after Lenin's death, but there were other contenders for power and intense debate about the direction the Soviet Union should take. Trotsky wanted to avoid the possibility of dictatorship which he feared was too often the consequence of a revolution. He wanted to extend the Russian revolution into other countries, a so-called 'Permanent Revolution'. He wanted to enforce strict discipline over the peasants and the workers, much as he had done over the Red Army during the Civil War, in order to move towards a communist society. Stalin, by contrast, advocated 'Socialism in one country' where 'world revolution' was abandoned in favour of building up Russia and the other Soviet states. The best method for the development of Russia's economy was also a subject of debate. Trotsky, Zinoviev and Kamenev wanted to bring the NEP to an end (to reduce prices, unemployment and some lingering food shortages), but Bukharin argued that the NEP would continue to enrich the peasants, increase consumer demand and stimulate all other aspects of the economy. They had already learned that conflict with the peasants would lead to disaster. In the debates, the protagonists appealed to a wider audience, and in this, Stalin was able to control personnel. His authority over party membership meant that he could remove opponents. His followers owed their success and positions to him, and they tended to be loyal. In 1922, his *Rabkhrin* was given the task of purging the party. As Party Secretary he also controlled the agendas of meetings. Each of Stalin's appointments in themselves seemed unimportant, but collectively they gave Stalin immense power over the provinces (the Commisar of Nationalities), the party membership, the appointments of the highest levels of the party and the bureaucracy (Party General Secretary and *Rabkhrin*), as well as sitting on the *Politburo*, the inner circle of the country's all-powerful party itself. His task as head of the *Orgburo* gave him control of the execution of decisions by the *Politburo*.

Stalin's struggle for the *Politburo* was primarily with Trotsky

It seems unlikely that Stalin was following any preconceived plan to take power. It seems that Stalin was engaged in a struggle and it only became clear that he would emerge triumphant near the end. Trotsky was the chief rival. He described Stalin as a 'dull mediocrity' and his strong basis of support in the army made him powerful. He was a great organiser but he was arrogant and treated others with disdain. He lost patience easily but as an intellectual he was a formidable opponent in debates. He tended to neglect the forging of political alliances and personal friendships that he could use. When he fell ill, he lacked the presence of his former years and was outmanoeuvred. However, in 1924, Kamenev and Zinoviev regarded Trotsky as 'too ambitious' and possessed of 'too much personality'. They feared he would carry out a coup with the army and saw him as 'a potential Bonaparte'.

Stalin engineered the fall of Trotsky

Kamenev, Zinoviev and Stalin accused Trotsky of being a Menshevik at heart (as he had only joined the Bolsheviks in 1917). Further, they accused him of being a critic of Lenin, which, against the background of the Lenin cult, was tantamount to heresy. Trotsky, eagerly protesting his loyalty to the party, declared that he accepted the will of the party which could not be wrong. While Kamenev, Zinoviev and Stalin formed the triumvirate against Trotsky, Trotsky failed to use the Political Testament against Stalin or use the army against his detractors. Krupskaya had made the Testament available to Kamenev and Zinoviev, but they suppressed it because of Lenin's criticisms of them. Trotsky was dismissed from the post of Commissar for War against a background of bitter recriminations. Stalin ensured that delegates at the party congress of 1924 voted on the side of the triumvirate.

Stalin defeated Kamenev and Zinoviev

Stalin then turned his attention against Kamenev and Zinoviev. He allied himself with Bukharin on the issue of continuing the NEP. His policy of 'socialism in one country' also proved popular with the party, and the other members of the *Politburo*, Rykov and Tomsky. Kamenev and Zinoviev called for the ending of the NEP and a tough line against the peasants, but Stalin's control of the party delegates meant that he won every vote. In 1926 Kamenev and Zinoviev joined Trotsky to form the United Opposition, whilst Stalin's side called itself the Moderates. The Moderates condemned the pursuit of world revolution (Trotsky's slogan) and condemned Kamenev and Zinoviev for doubting Lenin's call for revolutionary action in October 1917. The sections of the Political Testament which criticised these men were published. In 1927, the United opposition were expelled from the party. Trotsky was exiled to Mongolia and in 1929 was deported to Turkey. His continued criticism of Stalin outside of the USSR led to his assassination by Stalinist agents in Mexico in 1940.

Stalin used supporters to turn against the rest of the _Politburo_

Stalin claimed that the expulsions were the will of the party which he, as the General Secretary, must carry out. All leading communists agreed that the party could not be wrong and if the party decided that they should go, they were willing to accept its judgement. None wanted to be accused of factionalism or of being right-wing opportunists – all were determined to show their left-wing credentials and accept the people's will. Stalin used this to his advantage. He filled the vacant _Politburo_ places with his own supporters. Molotov became Foreign Minister, Voroshilov took over as War Commissar, and another Stalinist, Kalinin Kaganovich was appointed to the Central Committee of the Party and Kirov was made head of the party in Leningrad. In 1928, Stalin then condemned the NEP and advocated massive industrialisation with force to compel the peasants to co-operate with the state. The following year, Bukharin found himself outvoted by the array of Stalinists, and, with Rykov and Tomsky, was thrown out of the party. Stalin had succeeded because, as Issac Deutscher pointed out, Stalin always appeared to be going along with the majority. However, he created the majorities using his powers to appoint personnel.

The definition of Stalinism

Stalin secured power by political intrigue. His control of the party machinery gave him, indirectly, control of the state. He soon established a personal control of the state and was its unchallenged dictator. He scrapped NEP and began a process of collectivisation in agriculture and rapid industrialisation. When groups or individuals stood in his way, he unleashed the terror of the purges. Stalin ordered the execution of thousands of people and Stalinism is a term associated with a rigid dictatorship based on terror. Stalin murdered not only his opponents, but also many of his own supporters to 'encourage' the others to be obedient. As Stalin said: 'Ivan the Terrible's only mistake was not to have killed ALL his enemies'. Stalin was eager to ensure no rebellions or disobedience to his will, but this may not just have been a political objective: he may also have been suffering from paranoia. Whatever the psychological dimensions, his political objective, to modernise Russia, was pursued regardless of the human cost. He commanded a curious loyalty: partly a devotion to Lenin and communism, as well as a new cult of Stalin as leader, and partly through fear (fear of failure, of letting down 'the people', or fear of the system which was so unforgiving). Historians generally agree that Stalin did succeed, in a fashion, to turn Russia into a modern industrialised state, but at a terrible and unjustifiable cost. It could be argued that Russia could have modernised without any purges at all. Russia's armed forces, for example, were considerably weaker as a result of the purges, not stronger (they were beaten by the tiny Finnish defence force in the 'Winter War' of 1939–40, and almost defeated by the Nazis in 1941–42). Stalin ultimately presided over victory against the Nazis, the capture of large parts of eastern Europe, and the development of atomic weapons which led to a Cold War.

The Government	The Party
Sovnarkom 15 members under Lenin formed the 'Cabinet' of the government.	*Politburo* 7–9 members chosen by the Central Committee. Lenin presided over it. Under Stalin, the *Politburo* replaced the *Sovnarkom*.
Central Executive Committee Elected by the Congress of *Soviets*. A legislative body in theory, in fact it had little power.	**Central Committee** 30-40 members which ran the country when the Congress did not meet. It voted on Party issues but had no power compared to the *Politburo*.
All-Russian Congress of *Soviets* Elected delegates (weighted to favour the cities), who had little power – largely symbolic.	**Congress** Members were drawn from cities and regional branches of the Party. This body elected members to the Central Committee and *Politburo* and until Stalin's era could debate issues (although factions were banned and their were restrictions of loyalty).
Provincial and City *Soviets* An administrative body which fed issues to the hierarchy above.	**Provincial and City Party branches** Party leaders at this level were groomed for service in the hierarchy of the Party and their opinions were canvassed as 'grass roots' views. However, Party leaders at this level operated like Mafia bosses, exploiting favours and patronage from ambitious Soviet citizens.
Local *Soviets* Even at the local level, only members of the Communist Party could be elected to the *Soviet*. Executed the decisions of the bodies above.	**Local Party branches** Membership of the Party was a passport to better jobs or entry into local government and administration. Members at this level had no power.

Figure 5. The Soviet Government.

Tutorial

Progress questions
1. How far was Lenin responsible for the emergence of Stalin and Stalinism?
2. Is there any justification in the view that Stalin aimed to fulfil communist values?
3. What was the function and effects of the cult of Lenin?

Seminar discussion
Why have assessments of Stalin's rise differed so widely? How can contemporaries have so misjudged the real Stalin? Do the views of the 1920s illustrate that Stalin was the product of the communist system established by Lenin, or a strong leader in his own right?

Practical assignment
Account for the rise and fall of Trotsky as a communist leader. Construct an essay plan for this question. Try to balance the amounts you would cover on the rise and fall. Remember it is important to set the details of Trotsky's own skills and decisions with the context of the period as a whole. You may find it easier to tabulate the information you have with a column on Trotsky's skills and successes, his failures and mistakes, and the intervention of others or circumstances outside his control.

Study tips
1. The problem in trying to assess Lenin is that his reputation has been obscured by ideology. The best method for reaching an objective verdict is to judge him on his actions and his legacy.
2. Be aware that the idea of continuity between Lenin and Stalin is a contentious area. Examine the sections on historiography to gain a clearer picture of the debate and use a bullet point list to assess the similarities and differences between them.

10

Stalin's Economic Programme

One-minute summary – The priority for Stalin was to strengthen the Soviet Union. Although Lenin had agreed with Trotsky that Russia could not survive alone against the West, Stalin managed to persuade the *Politburo* that Lenin had really intended Russia be strengthened first, before an onslaught against the West. Stalin spoke of 'Mother Russia', appealing to nationalist sentiment rather than any abstract concept of internationalism. It was a case of 'work for Russia's stability, not the world's instability'. Stalin's economic policy consisted of two strands: collectivisation of agriculture and rapid industrialisation. The first would pay for the second. The method was to use force and drive forward the two policies. Economic strength would ensure Russia's survival as a 'great power', a policy pursued by Sergei Witte at the turn of the century. Marxist theory seemed to have been abandoned. Stalin's policies were pursued regardless of the cost and there was a great deal of human suffering. Unlike the development of the West, which had occurred in response to demand and under the control of entrepreneurs, the Soviet approach was entirely state directed and was known as a 'command economy'. The weakness of this approach was that it was inefficient, and gave little incentive to the workforce. The system eventually ground to a halt in the later twentieth century, causing the Soviet Union's collapse.

In this chapter you will learn:

▶ Stalin's collectivisation of agriculture
▶ the successes and failures of the five year plans
▶ the effects of Stalin's economic policies
▶ the cost of the policies.

Stalin's collectivisation of agriculture

Stalin's aims were to strengthen Russia
Stalin wanted to match the West in terms of industrial development. The main reasons for pursuing a policy of rapid change were:

▶ To increase Russia's military strength (for defensive, or offensive purposes).

▶ To achieve economic self-sufficiency (especially to reduce imported manufactured goods from the West).

▶ To increase grain supplies (to reduce reliance on the Russian peasantry and therefore reduce their political bargaining power).

▶ To create a communist society of obedient proletarians (only 28% of the population could be classed as 'workers' in 1928).

▶ To establish himself as the undisputed leader of Russia.

▶ To improve standards of living (to demonstrate to the world the benefits of living in a communist society).

The 'agricultural problem' was as political as it was economic

Russia's industrial base was small compared with Europe and its exports were simply unable to pay for the import of plant, machinery and other industrial equipment. Western powers were also unwilling to invest in communist Russia which had a history of bad debts, conflict and collapse. As a result, the only way to achieve industrial development was to export more agricultural produce, particularly grain. However, Russian agriculture also had to supply the growing populations of the cities, and Stalin believed that these two targets could not be met under the existing system of NEP which enriched the farmers, but not the state to a sufficient degree. Ninety-six per cent of land was privately owned and Stalin wanted to see the peasants brought under state control. This indicates that Stalin's approach to agriculture was not simply economic, but also political. Food production under NEP had exceeded the 1913 levels in 1925 and ended the shortages: it simply wasn't necessary to collectivise unless the government wanted to squeeze more of a surplus from the farmers.

The collectivisation of agriculture had economic and political dimensions

Initially the government tried to increase the grain surplus by taxing the farmers on the basis of money payments rather than in grain quotas as they had done since 1917. Private traders were suppressed so that farmers had to pay their grain to the state at low prices. However, the farmers realised that greater returns were possible if they produced less, fed surplus grain as fodder to their livestock and waited until prices increased on the market. Stalin's response was to send out the requisitioning squads, as the communists had done in the days of War Communism. Nevertheless, the grain yields fell and rationing was introduced in the cities. Stalin, angry that the farmers could hold the government to ransom, believed collectivisation would make it easier to control and monitor the people. He also believed that collectivisation would turn the peasants from independent small farmers into landless proletarians, ready to take their place in the new factories he intended to build. Any profits they produced would be siphoned into the state's coffers. The system of bringing people into collective farms would not be voluntary. Land units would be brought together, mechanisation introduced, and uniform working hours and practices would be enforced. Peasants would be moved into 'socialist agrotowns', large settlements, and be sent out into the fields in buses. Their children would remain in crèches and schools undergoing a communist education.

Stalin rushed ahead with collectivisation

There were three types of collective farm: the *Toz* (where farmers kept their land but shared machinery and practices such as sowing and harvesting), the *Sovkhoz* (a farm run by the state where they were paid wages) and the *Kolkhoz* (a community of 50–100 people run by an approved committee). In November 1929, Stalin began enforced collectivisation along the lines already practiced in the Urals in 1928. Unwilling to accept any resistance to his methods, Stalin wanted to press ahead rapidly even though there were not enough tractors or harvesters, and not enough time to organise the farmers. It is likely that the sliding yields and the worsening shortages in the cities prompted Stalin to act. Realising that he would meet considerable opposition, Stalin declared that there was a deliberate conspiracy by middle class farmers against the regime. He condemned the *Kulaks* and called for their 'liquidation as a class'. There was, of course, no such thing as a *Kulak* class, but the slogan of 'class enemy' had become a familiar term of abuse to conveniently explain away all sorts of problems in communist society.

Dekulakisation was the policy of the activists

Stalin hoped that poorer peasants would betray the richer farmers, but he had not expected that they would, in fact, support them. Better-off farmers sold some of their equipment to escape punishment, local party officials even supported them and condemned the demands for collectivisation. Stalin responded by recruiting 25,000 urban activists, who, after two weeks' training, descended in large numbers with police and OGPU (secret police) backing. Quotas were drawn up for the number of *Kulaks* to be arrested, even if they did not exist – they were to be found amongst the rural population. The *Kulaks* were either expelled and resettled on poor land, exiled to Siberia to forced labour camps (*gulags*), or shot as counter-revolutionaries. Ten million people were forced into labour camps and set to work on punishment projects, such as forest clearance, canal building and road construction. Whole villages were condemned as *Kulaks* and the title became a convenient badge to remove any opposition at all, regardless of their wealth or status. Propaganda broadcast that the *Kulaks* were enemies of the people who should be condemned. Children were encouraged to inform on their neighbours or even their parents.

The successes and failures of the five year plans

The targets were ambitious

The aim of the five year plans was to drive forward the industrialisation of the Soviet Union. For some, this mission took on the connotations of a quasi-religious crusade and the language of war was frequently used to generate enthusiasm: it was a 'class war' against 'class enemies' in the West, with 'fronts' and 'campaigns'. The basis of the plans was the setting of targets at every level, and quarterly during each year. Failure to achieve targets was a criminal offence, and success could bring bonuses. The five year plan targets were worked out by the 1921 central planning committee known as Gosplan, and the 1928 Party Congress instructed Gosplan to set up the first plan in 1928. The aim was to create an advanced industrialised state, with an increase in agricultural production by 130% and an industrial gross output 236% higher than the 1927–28 figures. Gross output was based on the 'A industries' of iron, coal and steel, and the 'B industries' of consumer goods, although the A industries were to be given the priority.

The promises were attractive

The first five year plan was designed to appeal to the young idealists of the party, the patriotic and the workers. Russia was to emerge as a strong power from the plan. Full employment was promised. There would be other benefits such as personal advancement, material improvements in wages, educational and technical skills and better careers.

The reality of the planning did not match the promises

In fact, the plan was badly conceived. The targets were impossible and over ambitious, and it strongly suggests that the motive was only partly economic. Trade Union leaders were warned not to interfere in the planning, but to focus on maximising productivity, the plan directors answered solely to the party leaders, and they reported directly to Stalin. However, there were overlaps and party officials interfered at every level. Propaganda concealed the failures of the plans and the propaganda message was spread to the West. At a time when the Great Depression was convulsing Europe and America, Stalin announced the completion of the first plan a year ahead of schedule. High prestige projects were begun, including the Moscow underground, the steel centre of Magnitogorsk and the massive Moscow-Volga Canal. They were designed to show the West that the workers did not need capitalism to achieve extraordinary feats. But these stunts concealed the darker reality of central planning. Those that failed to meet targets were being purged or sent off to labour camps. Fear generated corruption: in extreme cases factories that were producing 'millions' of goods had never been built, and figures achieved on paper had no basis in reality.

Consequences of the plans were mixed

The drive for heavy industry left the consumer sector neglected and the standard of living of the Soviet citizen fell accordingly. Food shortages were still prevalent in 1953, and according to Robert Conquest, Russia's index of standard of living was still that of Britain's in 1928. Depending on the criteria used to measure standard of living (such as household goods and spending power), it could be argued that Russians barely improved beyond even this. Even late in the Soviet Union's history, waiting lists for cars, queues for groceries and acute shortages of even basic consumer goods were common. Workers worked long hours for low pay. Productivity was low as a large workforce was guaranteed a job under the Soviet system. As a result, there was great inefficiency. At the Hotel Tashkent, there were dozens of staff for virtually no guests, three people operated one elevator and each corridor was served by an army of bored and underemployed cleaners (who had no cleaning materials beyond a mop and a bucket of cold water). The quality of Soviet goods was notoriously bad. In the Stalinist *gulags* (labour camps), 30 million slaves (*zeks*) were 'employed' by the secret police. Workers had no right to strike, no absenteeism was permitted and dissent could land a person in a *gulag*. A new elite emerged: the party members accrued all the benefits of the 'former people' prompting Orwell's ironic remark in *Animal Farm* (1945) that in the Soviet Union everyone 'is equal, it's just that some...are more equal than others'.

There were some achievements but they must be qualified

The five year plans set up new industries all over Russia and in ten years it moved up the industrial league table. The first plan increased steel production by one third, whilst coal and iron output doubled. Machine making, metal working, transport and communications were improved in the second plan. Above all, it created a more powerful MIC (Military-Industrial Complex). The second and third five year plans were focused on rearmament and the establishment of many strategic railway lines suggest Stalin had more than economic development for its own sake in mind in the mid-1930s. In terms of ranking, and taking the 1914 positions compared with the 1935 positions, the USSR moved from 5th (of the top five) in Europe in coal production to the 3rd, from the 4th (of four) to the second in iron ore extraction, and from 3rd in steel production to the second. According to Lionel Kochan, Stalinist Russia increased its overall production figures by 1939 four times more than in 1914. Yet in every case, the Soviet Union was behind Germany and it lagged well behind the United States. For all its promises, and all the brutality, the communists' economy still did not match the leading capitalist systems. Many targets were simply not met. Even steel production increased only marginally in the third plan. Robert Conquest believes that more could have been done with more humanity (especially as the purges threw Gosplan into chaos in 1938), whilst Martin Macauley argues that Russia was more powerful as a nation, but little was gained – only the party was more effective than before.

The effects of Stalin's economic policies

There was bitter resistance from the farmers

Farmers resisted in a variety of ways. Armed resistance was common. On several occasions, the OGPU or party officials were forced to call in the Red Army and they were sometimes forced to deploy heavy weapons. Collectivised livestock was liberated from *Kolkhoz* farms, women mounted demonstrations, crops were burned and animals killed in a desperate effort to keep them out of the hands of the state. Twenty-five to thirty per cent of all cattle, pigs and sheep were destroyed. Wild rumours began to circulate in the atmosphere of terror: it was feared that old people were to be burned and that women were to be routinely defiled. With the countryside descending into chaos, Stalin cynically backtracked in March 1930, allowing farmers to return to their farms to sow and harvest their food. He blamed the over-enthusiasm of young activists for the troubles. Then, in 1931, with the harvest in, the farmers were forced back into their collectives. The summer of 1931 was one of drought and, despite the export of grain to pay for industrial development, production levels had fallen. The result was famine.

Livestock losses, 1929–33 (millions)

Livestock	Population, 1929	Population, 1933
Cattle	70	34
Horses	33	15
Sheep and goats	146	42
Pigs	26	9

The Famine of 1932–34 cost millions of lives

Robert Conquest has suggested that as many as seven million people died from the famine of 1932–34. No exact figures are available because Stalin's regime denied the famine had ever occurred. Foreign journalists were kept away from the stricken areas and shown model collective farms. Scraps of evidence appeared in the years after Stalin's regime, and there were even reports of cannibalism in Siberia. Yet the worst affected area was Ukraine. There seems to have been a deliberate policy to break the most independent minded of all the Soviet states, and the vast peasant population within it. Brutal requisitioning gangs went in search of food hoards and extracted grain from the region, even though its people were starving. Due to the inefficiency of the regime, some foodstuffs were left rotting at railway sidings, yet those who tried to get at the stocks were shot down. In 1932, a ten-year prison term was decreed for anyone stealing state property and this was soon converted to the death penalty. Those who tried to flee to the cities were prevented by the imposition of internal passports: a return to the strictures of Tsarism. By the end of 1936, 90% of farmers were in collectives and although production levels improved, they did so very gradually. Meat production only regained its pre-1929 level in 1953, the year Stalin died. Farmers exercised a form of passive resistance. They had little incentive to work as the promised profits never materialised. Farmers were permitted small plots and it is estimated that these accounted for 52% of Russia's vegetables, 57% of fruit, 70% of meat and 71% of milk.

The cost of the policies

There were many contrasts in workers' conditions: Stakhanov and propaganda

Workforce discipline may have been harsh but the labour problem of the Soviet Union was not solved. There was a great deal of migration by workers, absenteeism and a tragic lack of technical training that resulted in damage to machinery. Bribery and corruption were rife, and there was a flourishing black market. The propaganda machine was used to conceal the reality and Alexei Stakhanov was singled out as an ideal type of Soviet worker. Using a number of assistants in a carefully arranged set up, Stakhanov cut 102 tons of coal in a five hour shift, sixteen times the normal rate. He was granted a special apartment, increased wages and special privileges at clubs. Konstantin Petrov, a Party official who had arranged Stakhanov's achievement then challenged others to beat his record. Stalin applauded the movement to beat records, a 'recordmania'. Critics were warned that any slander would be construed as making them 'vile enemies of the people'. Those that resisted the new drive for productivity were labelled as saboteurs. New higher targets were set from above, but it is clear that this was a carefully orchestrated propaganda coup. The typical life of a worker was long hours, little incentive, low pay, few consumer goods, shortages and monotony. Expressions of discontent were forbidden and there were no rights.

The rural population

The farmers were permanently alienated from the regime and they had little incentive to work for it. There was a great deal of hostility to the system. Livestock losses took years to recover (although the Second World War also resulted in large losses). Collective farm directors were worse than the Tsarist landlords in that they had more power and the demands of the quotas imposed an annual tyranny on the workforce. The standard of living was lower than in Witte's day and farmers remained on half the earnings of urban workers. Purely in terms of a standard of living, the peasants had been better off under the Tsars. No five year plan target for agriculture was ever achieved. The first plan, the government admitted, achieved only 58% of the targets. The second achieved 62%, the third was interrupted by the war and the fourth (from 1945–50) achieved 89% (although the targets were lowered). In the 1980s, Russia was still buying grain from the United States because it was so inefficient, and Eastern Bloc agriculture remained backward compared with the mechanisation of the West.

Tutorial

Progress questions

1. What was the purpose of Stalin's five year plans?
2. How did Stalin deal with opposition in the countryside?
3. How successful were the five year plans?

4. How justified was Stalin's claim to have continued Lenin's wishes in the economy?

Seminar discussion
1. Could more have been achieved in the Soviet economy in the 1930s?
2. What reasons can be given for Stalin's determination to destroy the *Kulaks* as a class?

Practical assignment
Using the tabulated information below, construct an appropriate graph and comment on the achievements of the economic Soviet plans. The figures in brackets indicate the targets as laid down at the start of each plan.

	1913	1928 (Plan I)	1932 (Plan I)	1933 (Plan II)	1937 (Plan II)	1940 (Plan III)
Electric power (billion kwh)	1.9	5	13.5 (22)	16.4	36.2 (38)	48.3
Coal (million tons)	29.1	35.5	64.4 (75)	76.3	128 (152.5)	165.9
Pig iron (million tons)	4.2	3.3	6.2 (10)	7.1	14.5 (16)	14.9
Steel (million tons)	3.5	3.4	4.4 (10.4)	5.1	13.0 (17)	13.1
Machine tools (thousands)	1.5	2	19.7	21	48.5	58.4
Sugar (million tons)	1.35	1.28	0.83	1	2.42	2.17
Cotton (million metres)	2582	2678	2694	2732	3448	3954

Total Industrial Potential of the Powers in Relative Perspective, 1913-38 (after Kennedy, *The Rise and Fall of the Great Powers*, 1989) Britain in 1913 = 100.

	1913	1928	1938
Britain	100	108	154
United States	271	506	500
Germany	111	131	188
Russia	49	45	125

Study tips

1. Be aware of the difficulties presented by the statistics. The Communist Party routinely replaced statisticians to get the figures they wanted. The fact that they claimed to have achieved their targets one year before the completion of the first plan should remind us to be cautious.

2. Bear in mind Stalin's motives in the economic policy he pursued. He was trying to win a battle for leadership of the party, feed the cities, crush the resistance of the independent farmers and drive forward Russia's industrialisation, convinced that a struggle with the West was inevitable.

11

The Great Terror

One-minute summary – The most notorious aspect of Stalin's regime was the Great Terror. In the purges, millions of people perished. It is impossible to give accurate figures, but Stalin's system exhibited a cruelty and a scale of barbarism hitherto unprecedented in Russia's turbulent history. Torture of a psychological as well as a physical kind was common. The most cynical illustration of this was the Show Trials, where public figures confessed to crimes they had not even committed in the hope of saving others. The purges were kept secret from the outside world and even the people of the Soviet Union would deny the excesses themselves. There was a mixed reaction: many hoped that a devotion to the regime would save them, but, tragically, it often did not. Where news leaked out, communist devotees would condemn the information as capitalist propaganda. Only in 1956, after Stalin's death, did the Soviet regime acknowledge the brutalities, but no one was convicted. In a shocking contrast to the fate of the Nazi leaders, the perpetrators of the Soviet crimes against humanity, including Stalin, did not pay for their atrocities.

In this chapter you will learn:

▶ Stalin's motives
▶ the purpose of the Show Trials
▶ the scale and intensity of the Great Terror
▶ the effects of the Terror
▶ the historical debate about this issue.

Stalin's Motives

Communism was intrinsically violent

The purges were not carried out in a period of crisis as had happened in previous cases. Lenin's concern that 'fellow travellers' had joined the Bolshevik Party in 1921 (and who might cause the Revolution to deviate from Lenin's plans) led to a purge of the party, but offenders were expelled rather than murdered. Having said that, the communist conception of revolution was a violent and bloody approach to politics. Lenin despised compromise and the Bolsheviks spoke in the language of war. Action and bloodshed was an intrinsic part of communist philosophy. In the structure of the state, there was still more inequality and repression. The Cheka was a brutal organisation that killed and tortured freely. In the Civil War, 'class enemies' had been executed without trial, and during the requisitioning of war communism, Lenin himself had endorsed the hanging of peasants who offered resistance. However, with the exception of the attacks on the *Kulaks*, there seems to have been no economic motive for the atrocities. The purges were political in the sense that they were designed to establish and reinforce Stalin's position as undisputed leader of the Soviet Union.

Stalin's motives were negative but he could justify his actions

The purges were designed to remove opposition and crush any dissatisfaction with his rule. Nevertheless, there is considerable debate about Stalin's personal reasons for unleashing the terror. Was it a cold and rational decision which dovetailed with his policy of securing power, or was it the product of mental instability or even paranoia? His position, it could be argued, was insecure. He had only narrowly assumed power and there were many rivals. The lack of progress in the Soviet Union also made the party, and therefore Stalin's position, unstable. The peasants had been on the verge of a full scale revolt in 1921, and Stalin had caused considerable unrest in the provinces with his policy of collectivisation and his war on the *Kulaks*.

The Soviet Union was seething with discontent

Not only was the countryside in turmoil, but people in the cities were angry at working conditions, particularly the poor pay and long hours. There was anger at the high handedness of the secret police. Members of the Communist Party were anxious about the violence of the collectivisation policy. Nadeza Allilueva, Stalin's wife, committed suicide in despair at the war on the farmers and Stalin's string of affairs. Stalin's biographer, Edward Radzinsky, wrote in 1997 that Stalin had the affairs to spite Nadeza. There is disagreement about Stalin's reaction to his wife's suicide: did he see it as a betrayal? His daughter, Svetlana, wrote that 'something snapped inside' him and he became introverted, trusting no one. Meanwhile, it was clear that local Party officials were refusing to carry out actions against the *Kulaks*. Party leaders therefore implemented a *chisti*, or cleansing of the organisation in December 1932. Membership cards were withdrawn from 22% of the Party. The explanation given officially was that 'turncoats' had allied themselves to 'bourgeois elements'. Ryutin, the former Moscow Party secretary, published a 200 page condemnation of Stalin as the 'evil genius of the Revolution'. Ryutin was arrested but not executed, despite Stalin's protests. Senior members of the Party began to discuss slowing down the pace of industrialisation, to focus on standards of living for the workers and to moderate the policy of collectivisation. Others called for the OGPU to be brought under Party control.

The death of Kirov initiated the Terror

At the 1934 Party Conference, Kirov received more applause than Stalin on the question of reform and this convinced Stalin that Kirov was a potential opponent. Kirov expressed the widely held view that the tensions caused by forced industrialisation needed to be addressed. The Congress decided that Stalin and

Kirov should be given equal rank as party secretaries. On 2 December 1934, at this critical moment in history, Kirov was assassinated. The assassin, Leonid Kikolayev, was caught and was identified as a disaffected member of the party. All the killer's accomplices were executed without trial on 'suspicion'. Kirov's NKVD bodyguards were sentenced to short periods in Siberia, but received special privileges (although they were all later executed). Had Kirov been murdered on Stalin's orders and were his henchmen all killed because they knew too much and might implicate Stalin? Stalin initiated a purge to remove the evident 'threat' to the party. Kamenev and Zinoviev were arrested and imprisoned on the charge of opposing Stalin, and for the 'moral and political responsibility' for the death of Kirov. Stalin condemned their past 'repression' of the Russian people. The charges were fabrications. Other party members who gave 'opposition to the Party' were either executed or imprisoned. By January 1935, thousands had been arrested for their 'part' in the murder of Kirov. As the Stalinist devotees went about their work, any critics were labelled as 'opposition' and either murdered or sent to the Lublianka (prison for political criminals).

The Show Trials

The Trials gathered pace

In 1936, there were a series of Show Trials. Each condemned prisoner confessed and gave the names of other 'criminals'. The world was stunned by the revelations. The first trial in August that year was the 'Trial of the Sixteen', the leftist supporters of Trotsky and Zinoviev. They were accused of political murders and 'plotting to overthrow the state'. All confessed and all were shot. The head of the NKVD, as the secret police were now known, Yagoda, was reluctant to carry out the sentences against the 'guilty' and he was replaced by Yezov, an enthusiastic Stalinist. The pace of the trials increased correspondingly. In January 1937, the 'Trial of the Seventeen' took place. This was aimed at party members including Bukharin and Rykov, the Commander in Chief of the army (a hero of the Civil War), Tachachevsky, and the Commander of the navy, Orlov. An atmosphere of fear developed; people were afraid of traitors and spies but accepted that firm action was needed. In February 1937, Sergei Ordzhonikidze, a leading light in the Commissariat of Heavy Industry, confronted Stalin about the purges. Stalin gave him the choice of suicide and a state funeral or being shot with no state funeral. The official report was that Ordzhonikidze had died of 'heart failure' and he received a state funeral.

The purge of the armed forces

In June 1937, the trial of the armed forces leaders took place. All the condemned were accused of spying for Germany and Japan. Obligingly, the Gestapo provided 'evidence' and the men were shot. Three of the five army marshals, 14 out of 16 army commanders, 13 out of 15 generals and two out of every three officers above the rank of colonel were killed. Thirty-five thousand were imprisoned or shot. This purge weakened the armed forces severely. In the Russo-Finnish War of 1939–40, Russian formations did very badly and the cost was high. When the Germans invaded the Soviet Union in 1941, the Russian armed forces had still not recovered and they were defeated.

The purge of the Party followed
The 'Trial of the Twenty One', the fourth, followed swiftly and was focussed against the 'Rightists' after being implicated in the third trial. Tomsky committed suicide to avoid the firing squad but all the others were shot. What the outside world, and even the people of the Soviet Union, did not know was that each confession was wrung from the accused by torture and threats against their families. Promises of pardons were made in return for confessions, but these promises were not kept. Many of the victims still believed that the Party must be right and they were prepared to sacrifice themselves for the 'greater good'. Ninety-eight out of 139 members of the Seventeenth Party Congress, where Kirov had been given equal rank to Stalin, were murdered, and 1,100 out of 1,966 Party delegates were arrested.

The Great Terror

Murders on a massive scale and a society that controlled itself
Following the trials, the purges were turned on the people of the Soviet Union. Sentences were passed, millions were imprisoned and perhaps as many as seven million were executed. If one person was implicated then often his or her family members could also be purged. Thirty million people served in slave labour conditions in the labour camps. According to Robert Conquest, the population of the camps was between seven or eight million, but unlike Dmitiri Volkogonov, who believes that sixteen million worked in the camps and seven million died, Conquest estimates that one and a half million were executed, two million died in camps and seven million died of the famine. The total deaths, Conquest believes, amounted to twenty million.

Stalinist Russia was a land of fear
Fear pervaded the entire country and many denounced friends and neighbours in a scramble to appear loyal, and before others got in first. People spoke and behaved as the regime required, and many only allowed themselves to think the way the state permitted. If a person could demonstrate loyalty and not give himself or herself away, they could survive. The 'politically correct' words, slogans, behaviour and thoughts pervaded all aspects of Soviet life. Education, youth movements, culture, media, information, the armed forces, government and administration; all were subject to a totalitarian control. Totalitarianism operates not just from a hierarchical structure, with orders flowing downwards,

but requires the active participation of the masses, each one anxious to keep from criticism and conforming to the socially acceptable norms. It was this situation that George Orwell captured so brilliantly in his novel, *1984*, which was based on observations about Stalin's Russia.

Life in the *gulags* was harsh

NKVD agents arrested many Soviet citizens in the middle of the night and all came to fear the knock on the door. For those that were not immediately tortured and executed, a sentence in a slave labour camp was the norm. In the Arctic north, inadequate clothing and rations meant that many perished from the cold. Malnutrition, relentless hard work, and beatings were also common. On the White Sea Canal alone, it is estimated that 100,000 died. Some of the projects were heartbreaking because they were pointless. Those condemned to work on railway gangs across Siberia in the winter saw the surface layers melt in the summer, warping the railway lines and causing bridges to collapse. Stalin's instructions were that the railways were to be begun again and so the toil that had already cost thousands of lives began all over again. Mosquitoes and mud in the summer, freezing conditions in the winter and torture or death for any dissent: this was the lot of the *gulag* inhabitants.

The effects of the Terror

The results of the Terror were far reaching

If the political aim of the Terror had been to eliminate all opposition, then it was certainly achieved. Five thousand members of the Party were 'removed' and thousands of former Bolsheviks, including foreign members, were eliminated. A new Stalinist party replaced the old revolutionaries. However, as far as the armed forces were concerned, Stalin may have realised that with a European war imminent by 1939, the purges had gone too far. Moreover, industry was also suffering. Many of the skilled workforce were dead, accused of sabotage. Stalin must have known that the purges were acting contrary to his policy of industrialisation. Stalin was also afraid that the NKVD, who were carrying out the purges, were becoming too powerful.

In 1939, Stalin ordered the purge of the NKVD itself

'Yesov' disappeared, replaced by the more enthusiastic Beriav. Stalin accused the NKVD of acting against the Party will. He issued pardons to some, an act which made them grateful and more loyal. Nevertheless, some 23,000 NKVD men were killed by the end of the 1930s, according to Volkogonov.

The Terror was effective

All possible rivals had been eliminated. The Party was totally under Stalin's control and the Party was unchallenged until 1990. Expressions of loyalty had to be enthusiastic to ensure survival and a cult of Stalin emerged. This quasi-religious sentiment endorsed the view that Stalin was a genius who was always right. Tragically this situation is not unique, and dictatorships under Iraq's Saddam Hussein and North Korea's Kim Jong-il exhibited the same phenomenon of fear and leader-worship. To legitimise such personal and powerful rule, dictators appear to need the 'love' of the people, an enthusiastic devotion that ensures they will behave obediently as ordered. Stalin may have developed delusions about his power as he was surrounded by people eager to profess their fealty. At Party Conferences, applause for Stalin lasted for excessively long periods because each member of the audience did not want to be seen to be the first to stop clapping. Nevertheless, even after the war, Stalin feared internal enemies. Fearing that his doctors were Jewish conspirators (reflecting an anti-Semitism common amongst the people of the former Czarist Empire), he began a purge of his own medical staff. He died before it was complete.

The historical debate

The decisionists believe Stalin was central to the Terror

The historians of the West, and most recently, Robert Conquest, have shown that the Great Terror emanated from the very top. Stalin was the man who planned the purges and, as the leader with exclusive power, he orchestrated the apparatus of terror, directing the NKVD towards its targets. Stalin may have used the purges as a means to control his own party as much as the country. The Terror can be explained by examining Stalin's personality, and by looking at the system he set up. Alexander Solzhenitsyn, the famous dissident who fled to the West, saw a direct connection between Lenin and Stalin in the apparatus of the state. However, left-wing historians in the West refused to accept the 'decisionist' theory that Stalin was responsible.

The revisionists believe responsibility was more widely spread

J. Arch Getty blamed the Cold War atmosphere for distorting the Western view of the Soviet Union and he sought to distance Stalin from sole responsibility. He argued that Stalin had no blueprint for terror and, although he was in charge of the process, his personality defects do not explain the whole episode. At times, Stalin appeared to have little idea of what was actually happening, Getty suggested. The system developed a momentum of its own, driven forward by enthusiastic supporters. The chaotic nature of the Soviet Union meant that officials acted on their own initiative. The randomness of the arrests confirms that it was an irrational fear that impelled the Terror, rather than tight control. Sheila Fitzpatrick, Graeme Gill and Roberta Manning tend to agree with the line taken by Getty.

The solution is to combine the approaches

Until more records are released from the former Soviet Archives, it is difficult to be certain how much support there was for the Terror. It was certainly open to abuse. In the French Revolution, the *Grande Peu*, fear of internal enemies of the Revolution, had provoked mass hysteria and widespread murders. However, the organisation of camps in the Soviet Union, the thoroughness of the targeting and executions, and the sheer scale of the killing suggests more than a movement of panic. There can also be little doubt that Stalin was a deeply suspicious man who saw potential enemies everywhere.

Stalin's cult developed

Stalin offered the people of the Soviet Union, and more importantly, foreigners, a view that was carefully arranged to show the country and its leader in the best light. Stalin encouraged flyers to attempt new speed and altitude records. Mountaineers were challenged to climb previously inaccessible peaks, workers like Stakhanov were urged to work still harder. These individuals were made heroes of the Soviet Union, apparently moulded in the image of Stalin, the 'man of steel', himself. Stalin's image appeared everywhere, paintings were commissioned in the new 'socialist-realism genre' (showing heroic workers or Stalin as a towering leader), and sychophantic poetry was written. History books were rewritten to suit Stalin's tastes and he was given a more prominent role in the Revolution. After the war, the memoirs of Marshal Zhukov, the most talented commander of the Soviet Union, were rewritten to give Stalin more credit. Stalin's birthday greetings for his seventieth birthday lasted from December 1949 to August 1951! On a more sinister note, photographs of Stalin with Party leaders who were purged were subsequently 'doctored'. A photograph of 1925, showing nine leaders, was republished in 1939 showing only four and was captioned as if nothing had changed. For many ill-educated people, Stalin was the *vozhd* (saviour) who appeared as an icon in people's homes much as the old saints had done: no one protested openly, for obvious reasons.

Tutorial

Progress questions

1. Which aspects of Stalin's rule were 'totalitarian'?
2. Was there a 'social revolution' under Stalin?
3. Why do historians disagree about the Great Terror? What part has the personality cult played in the assessments?

Seminar discussion

Did the Terror help or hinder Stalin's other policies and ambitions?

Practical assignment

Compare the two sources below and answer the questions that follow:

Source A: J. Arch Getty, *The Origins of the Great Purges* (1985)

Western scholars have remained hypnotised by Stalin's cult of personality, and their obsession with him has led to studies of the Great Purges period that provided no detailed investigation of the poitical and institutional context. Rather than placing these events in these contexts, scholars have often discussed the Great Purges only against the background of Stalin's personality and categorised Stalinisim simply as the undisputed rule of an omniscient and omnipotent dictator. Contradictions and confusion are seen as manifestations of Stalin's caprice, and all too often the political history of the Stalin period has merely been the story of Stalin's supposed activities.

Source B: Robert Service, *A History of Twentieth Century Russia* (1997)

The Great Terror would not have taken place but for Stalin's personality and ideas. It was he who directed the state's punitive machinery against all those whom he identified as 'anti-Soviet elements' and 'enemies of the people'. Among his purposes was a desire to use his victims as scapegoats for the country's pain; and in order to sustain his mode of industrialisation he also needed to keep his mines, his timber forests and construction sites constantly supplied with slave labour. It was probably also his intention to take pre-emptive measures against any 'fifth column' operating against him in the case of war. These considerations, furthermore, fitted into a larger scheme to build an efficient Soviet state subservient to his personal dictatorship – and to secure the state's total control over society. Such was the guiding rationale of the Great Terrorist.

1. How far do these sources, and your wider knowledge, show that Stalin was 'brutal *and* effective' in his leadership of the Soviet Union?
2. In light of these sources, how important do you think 'personality' is in assessing the period of the Great Terror and the Stalin years in general?

Study tips

1. In George Orwell's novel, *1984*, a society is governed by an all-seeing and all-knowing character called Big Brother. However, Big Brother turns out to be a fiction so Orwell was suggesting that it was the system that was keeping people locked in subservience, not necessarily an actual leader. Society lived a self-regulating environment where everyone conformed. It is worth bearing this in mind when examining this period of Stalinist rule.
2. The death tolls are terrifying, but accurate records are not available. It is anticipated that more archives will be opened to inspection in the twenty-first century – look out for them.

3. Notice how historians are divided on this issue. The division is less absolute than it looks. All agree that Stalin had some responsibility and the degree of leadership seems irrelevant compared with the nature of the system. Look out for comparative questions and be able to identify the degree to which Stalinism owed its existence to Leninism.

12

Conquest and Subversion 1939–45

One-minute summary – When the Bolsheviks came to power, they refused to acknowledge any of Russia's debts or treaties. In 1919, they established the Comintern, or Communist International, an agency designed to spread world revolution via foreign communist parties. From the outset, the communists aimed to subvert the political structures of other countries and aimed to destroy the capitalist system of the West. Yet the weakness of the Soviet Union prevented any chance of world revolution. Under Stalin, greater loyalty to the Soviet Union was demanded, even of foreign communists. As war approached Stalin decided to throw in his lot with the Nazis to preserve peace and acquire parts of eastern Europe, but this was a reversal of an anti-fascist policy which had ended with Soviet support for republicans in the Spanish Civil War. However, in 1941, the Soviet Union was invaded and it bore the brunt of the Nazi war effort throughout the Second World War. Initial defeats, caused by Stalin's pre-war purges, were superseded by limited victories, before the full force of the Soviet total war effort secured final victory.

In this chapter you will learn:

▶ what the aims and activities of the Comintern were
▶ the reasons for the formation of the Nazi-Soviet Pact
▶ Stalin's wartime leadership.

The aims and activities of the Comintern

Lenin misjudged the attitude of other Europeans towards communism

The Comintern was set up in 1919 in Moscow with the specific aim of propagating revolution in other countries as part of a programme of world revolution. Despite the unrest caused the by the First World War, few in Europe rallied to the call of the Communist Party. Communists were blinded by their own idealism and ideology: they misinterpreted the unrest as dissatisfaction with capitalism, when it was purely a reaction to the circumstances thrown up by the war – such as shortages and heavy casualties. In Berlin, German communists, the Spartakists, were crushed by a combination of army personnel and legions of demobilised soldiers called Freikorps. Bavaria, or rather Munich, briefly declared itself a Soviet republic, but its activists were overwhelmed. Hungary, under the leadership of Bela Kun, was a Marxist state for four months before it fell too.

Lenin launched the Red Army in support of the workers

Whilst the Red Army set off to crush Poland (in a plan to roll westwards), Lenin organised the Second International in 1920. Delegates from 41 countries were invited and the Bolsheviks stage-managed an impressive performance. The aim was to bring the other European communists firmly under Lenin's control. He demanded that they adopt a Leninist approach (centralisation and greater discipline in the party), spread propaganda, organise cells for a forthcoming civil war, and submit all proposals for action to Moscow for approval. There was some resentment at this insistence, and the reputations of communist movements were damaged as each national population saw the communists as 'foreign' agents. At times, promised finances did not materialise from Moscow. The defeat of the Red Army in Poland also revealed how weak the Soviet Union really was. In 1923, this was illustrated by the Curzon Ultimatum. The British Foreign Secretary, Lord Curzon, demanded that communist propaganda being broadcast in south Asia should cease or there would be an end to the recently concluded Anglo-Soviet trade agreement. The activities were curbed. Soviet support for the British general strike in 1926, with a sum of £26,000, angered the British government but also discredited the British communists. The failure of the strike did little to allay fear and hostility towards the far left. In 1927, the British police launched the Arcos raid to arrest suspects of a Soviet spy ring.

An isolated Germany chose to co-operate with the Soviet Union

In 1922, Germany, which was still isolated after the First World War, concluded the Rapallo Treaty with the Russians. Although the Bolsheviks had spent considerable sums to overthrow the Weimar Republic of Germany, it was in the two countries' interests to co-operate. The German Army agreed to train the Russians in tank warfare and aviation, and in return, German units were permitted to train in Russia using tanks, poison gas and aircraft (which had been banned under the terms of the Treaty of Versailles). Germany also gave loans, and sold Russia heavy industrial goods. Russia gave the Germans the opportunity to build munitions and tanks, and the sale of its goods boosted the German economy at a difficult time.

Stalin ignored the Comintern

Stalin's rivalry with Trotsky, the advocate of world revolution, meant that the Comintern's efforts would not be looked upon favourably by Stalin. Stalin preferred to ignore the Comintern and focus on 'socialism in one country'. Stalin's views are most clearly illustrated in the case of China. The Comintern had helped in the founding of a Chinese Communist Party in 1921, but urged the fledgling organisation to work alongside nationalists in a front called the Goumindang. Chiang Kai-Shek was trained in Moscow as a potential leader of the front, but back in China he exhibited anti-communist tendencies. Stalin, in fact, backed Chiang Kai-Shek and not the communists because he believed Chiang Kai-Shek had more chance of taking power. However, in the end Stalin fully expected that

Chiang Kai-Shek would turn to the communists, who, in turn, would be taking their orders from Moscow. In fact, Chiang Kai-Shek attacked the Chinese communists in 1927, killing some 30,000, and he established himself as fully independent of the Soviet Union. Mao Zedong, the new Chinese communist leader, also broke the alignment with Moscow.

Stalin's attitude towards the Comintern and the orders he gave out reflected what was happening internally in the Soviet Union. Intellectuals were replaced as leaders of the foreign communist parties by more pliant working class candidates. European communists were ordered to attack the moderate left as 'social fascists' in the period 1930–32, as Stalin denounced the leftists in his struggle for power. The effect of this was to divide the anti-right wing movements at a crucial time. Hitler secured power partly as a result of divisions on the left (see Robert Johnson, *Hitler and Nazi Germany*, Studymates, 1999, 2001, 2004).

Stalin turned to diplomacy to improve the security of the Soviet Union
In 1934, Hitler signed a non-aggression pact with Poland, effectively ending the Treaty of Rappallo. The Nazis attacks on communists in Germany in 1933–34 indicated that Hitler saw the communists as his greatest threat. The change in Germany coincided with an improvement in relations with Western Europe and the United States. In December 1933, Soviet policy seemed to encourage the idea of 'collective security', the very concept the League of Nations had been promoting since 1919. In September 1934, the Soviet Union joined the League, but self-interest was the motive. Japan's annexation of Manchuria in 1931 and its aggressive nationalist tone that matched that of Germany, posed a threat on two fronts. In 1935, the USSR signed an agreement with France and Czechoslovakia, offering assistance to the Czechs. Again, this was self-interest at heart. The Czechs were a buffer against Germany and offered a southern flank against Poland.

The Spanish Civil War was a departure from self-interest
When the Spanish Civil War broke out in 1936, many in Europe saw it as a struggle between the right and left wings. Stalin knew that it would be impossible for Russia not to play a part in the conflict if the Soviet Union was to retain its credibility and if the policy of collective security against fascism was to mean anything. The war would also distract foreigners from any concern with Stalin's domestic policy, provide a useful propaganda ramp and perhaps even throw open the opportunity of defeating the Trotskyites (using NKVD men to eliminate them). Stalin sent token numbers of men (700 advisors), 650 modern planes, 400 armoured vehicles and 18,000 largely obsolete machine guns (with little ammunition). At first the instructions to the communists were to be moderate, but in 1937 Stalin urged the crushing of the anarchists and Spanish Trotskyite factions. Soviet advisors became more influential but the left was defeated by Franco and his fascist allies in 1939.

The formation of the Nazi-Soviet Pact, 1939

Stalin negotiated with both democratic and fascist states in 1939

Stalin believed that the best way of protecting the Soviet Union was to negotiate with both Hitler and the Western democratic states. He played no part in the dismemberment of Czechoslovakia in March 1939, but this was possibly because he had already begun secret negotiations with Hitler. Stalin seemed to be convinced that the Western powers would rather see Hitler attack the Soviet Union than themselves and he interpreted their non-intervention policy in the Spanish Civil War as evidence of their half-heartedness to stand up to the fascists (in fact, the League of Nations prevented intervention in the internal dispute of a nation state). Stalin also realised how weak his armed forces were after the purges and how a pact with the Nazis would secure territorial influence over the Baltic States, Poland and even Finland – the former Tsarist territories on the fringe of the Soviet Union. There was also, after all, a precedent of co-operation with Germany. In 1938 there had been a border clash between the Russians and the Japanese and a full-scale campaign took place between July and August 1939 which resulted in a Japanese defeat at Kalkhin Gol. Stalin hoped that Germany would be able to restrain its ally Japan. In August 1939, the Nazi-Soviet Pact was signed, bringing to an end the policy of 'collective security'.

Stalin's wartime leadership

Stalin's expansionism fulfilled the deal with the Nazis

In September 1939, the Germans invaded Poland and, in accordance with the secret clauses of the Nazi-Soviet Pact, the Red Army invaded from the east. On 29 September, Poland was partitioned between the two powers and ceased to exist. The NKVD arrived and deported thousands of Poles to the *gulags*, and, in a forest at Katyn, Polish army officers were secretly murdered. In November, Stalin then ordered the invasion of Finland. The Finns resisted fiercely. Their ski-borne troops ambushed the Soviet units which had become immobilised by freezing conditions. Russian infantry were hurled at the Finns in the hope of overwhelming them with sheer weight of numbers, but they were cut down in the snowdrifts by machine guns. The Germans observed how badly led the Russians were and how narrowly they secured their 'victory' (a ceasefire was signed in 1940). The Baltic States were the next to be invaded in March 1940 and they fell swiftly. Once again, the NKVD moved in and 1.2 million people were deported to Siberia. Romania's Bessarabia was annexed and thousands more deported. In line with the pact with Hitler, oil, rubber, copper and grain were shipped to Nazi Germany to crush Britain and France. Stalin had told the Politburo that he wanted conflict between Germany and the Anglo-French bloc to last as long as possible, so as to weaken the two sides

Operation Barbarossa took Stalin by surprise

Stalin was warned by spies, by Churchill and by Hitler's own speeches that the Soviet Union was Germany's next target, but Stalin refused to believe them all. A deserter who brought news of the date and time of the German attack was shot on Stalin's orders. However, on 21 June 1941, the Nazis unleashed Operation Barbarossa, the invasion of the Soviet Union. German troops (totalling 3.2 million) took on 170 Soviet divisions and threw them back in confusion. Stalin's response was to deny it had happened and he ordered Russian artillery not to fire on German units. In nine days, the Germans had taken Minsk and a whole Soviet Army Group was surrounded, losing 3,785 tanks and 440,000 men. Smolensk fell on 16 July with a further 300,000 prisoners. The Ukrainians and people of the Baltic States welcomed the Germans as liberators from Stalinist oppression. Nevertheless, the NKVD continued to murder any Soviet officers who escaped the German attacks and they evacuated the slave labourers eastwards.

Nazi atrocities soon changed the minds of the people

The Nazi obsession with rooting out the Jewish-Bolshevik threat to world civilisation meant that in the wake of the advancing German armies, thousands of commissars, Jews and 'social undesirables' were shot. Russian prisoners of war were treated little better than animals. The German offensive continued as planned. Kiev fell with an entire Russian army intact inside. However, resistance increased after the initial shock. Small groups of men and women would open fire, even when the odds were hopeless. The German soldiers began to feel that they were advancing into a limitless space, characterised only by increasingly fanatical resistance. Veterans of the Wehrmacht spoke of the headlong charges by Russian formations, blaring loudspeakers, and immense enemy casualties. On 14 October, the Germans had advanced to within 100 miles of Moscow and were battering a 600,000 strong Russian defence force with artillery, tanks and aircraft. There was panic in Moscow. Marshal Zhukov, a brilliant strategist, was transferred to the Moscow sector, and he told Stalin in no uncertain terms how he intended to conduct the defence of the city. Fear of the Nazis and of the Stalinist regime encouraged thousands to dig anti-tank ditches and lay mines on the approaches to the city.

The weather helped the resistance in Moscow

Snow fell as the Soviets prepared to meet the extended and exhausted German thrust to Moscow. The freezing temperatures certainly helped the Russians whose tanks were better suited to the conditions. Stalin also invoked the defence of 'Mother Russia' and historic characters to bolster the people's resolve. With just 14 miles to go, the Germans were checked by a combination of resistance and frozen tanks, weapons and equipment. They made one last effort on 1 December that reached within one mile of the city but Zhukov counter-attacked. News of Japan's attack on Pearl Harbor meant that the feared second front was less likely. Thousands of fresh troops could be transferred to fight the Germans in the West and their impending arrival released Zhukov from a purely defensive stance. As the Russian liberated territory they found murdered civilians and this spurred them on to revenge. The Germans were stopped 42 miles from the city.

Leningrad was besieged

Hitler wanted to avoid costly street fighting and so besieged Leningrad. Its 3 million inhabitants were gradually starved of food and medical supplies. In December 1941, 200,000 died of cold and hunger. Rodents, cats and horses were eaten and cannibalism developed. The siege lasted 900 days, and when it was lifted 900,000 had died.

The relocation of industry

The loss of resources was catastrophic but many industries were relocated. The Nazis occupied territory in which 45% of the population had lived, and where a third of the wheat fields lay. Half of the country's cattle and horses were lost to the Germans. However, despite the chaos of the retreat, many of the factories had been relocated in and beyond the Urals and 1,360 large war factories and 17 million people were moved in a vast migration eastwards. A million cattle were herded out of harm's way. All this was done in freezing winter conditions. Men were extracted from the farms, leaving women and old people to carry on the work and where there was an absence of horses for the ploughs, women dragged them by hand. Some factories were up and running within three months of the move eastwards. By July 1942, aircraft production exceeded that of 1941. Tank production doubled in 1942 and countless other munitions were produced on a gigantic scale.

Stalingrad was the turning point

On 23 August 1942, the Germans reached the river Volga, a few hundred miles from the Caucasus oilfields to the south east. At the city of Stalingrad, the Russians fought to hold the Germans back. A long, see-sawing street battle developed. Hand-to-hand fighting was common. Yet the Germans were being drawn into a battle of attrition, and weakening their flanks. The Russians attacked from north and south on 19 November and on 31 January 1943, the Commander of the German Sixth Army, von Paulus, surrendered what remained on his encircled forces. Ninety thousand men were made prisoners but many of them did not survive Soviet captivity. In addition, many of the Soviet casualties of the battle were victims of their own side. The NKVD routinely shot shirkers to encourage others to fight. Nevertheless, much of the Russian resistance was voluntary and self-sacrificial.

Stalin aimed to associate himself with victory

As the course of the war changed, Stalin gave himself a higher profile. He made himself Marshal of the Soviet Union after the victory at Stalingrad. Victory at Kharkov was attributed to the 'superiority of the ideology of Marx, Engels and

Lenin'. However, there was a darker side to the new ideological onslught. When the Germans had taken Kharkov, the population was 700,000 but it was half that when it was retaken in February 1943 (thousands had been taken as slave labour), but the NKVD killed many more. Thousands of tons of equipment was pouring into the Soviet Union from the West. Britain and America sent tanks, planes and trucks, food and ammunition. Two thirds of Red Army lorries were American-built by the end of the war and many seamen had risked their lives in the Arctic Convoys to get the material to the Russians. Stalin never acknowledged this support.

The Red Army assumed greater influence over the running of the war
Zhukov managed to persuade Stalin not to be premature in making attacks at Kursk, where there was a bulge in the German lines. On 5 July, the Germans launched their offensive called Citadel, and the battle lasted for days, but Zhukov marshalled his reserves, meeting each thrust, confident that his losses could be replaced as tank production reached 2,000 vehicles a month. The Germans, still at the end of an extended supply chain, could not replace their equipment as quickly. Stalin authorised other reforms at the suggestion of Zhukov. Guards units, once a feature of despised Tsarist forces, were revived. Officer cadets schools were reinstated. The Comintern, and the egalitarianism of the world revolution, was formally scrapped.

The war turned into one of atrocities
Three million Russians, Ukrainians and other nationalities had been deported to the Third Reich. Jews were herded into concentration camps and then murdered in their millions in the death camps. Thousands of villages had ceased to exist in western Russia, and as the German retreated they destroyed what was left. At Babyi Yar, near Kiev, the Nazis tried to exterminate the Jews as they went, and killed 100,000 in one of the largest single episodes of mass killing. Yet the Germans were also suffering the same fate as their victims. At Korsun, south of Kiev, eight German units were surrounded. They killed their own wounded in fear of Soviet revenge and then tried to escape, but they were caught and massacred. Twenty thousand were killed in the initial fighting, but scores more were hunted down in the forests and butchered. The NKVD continued to turn on its own side. Crimean Tartars were suspected of collaboration and deported to Siberia. Hundreds were hanged. Other Cossack minorities were packed off from their homelands, even though their menfolk were still fighting the Germans in the Ukraine. The Soviets established penal battalions who were forced to run into minefields to clear the way for the troops behind. Partisans assisted the Red Army behind German lines, but suffered heavy casualties as a result.

The Russians drove on to Berlin
The Red Army was better equipped and more numerous than the German forces by 1944. They drove the Germans out of Russia and paused on the Vistula. The

Poles in Warsaw, thinking the Soviet liberation of their capital from the Nazis was imminent, rose up in rebellion. But Stalin halted the troops, allowing the Germans to crush the Polish resistance. Once the Soviets arrived in East Prussia, discipline almost broke down. Women were raped, murdered and crucified with a brutal savagery unprecedented even by the standards of the twentieth century. Entire civilian populations were annihilated. Millions fled westwards. Thousands committed suicide. A British prisoner in Pomerania stated that *every* German women between 12 and 60 was raped by the Red Army. Solzhenitsyn testified that every man in his regiment regarded rape, and then the murder of the victim, as a combat distinction.

Berlin fell in May 1945
In the final battle for Berlin, resistance by the Germans was as determined as that shown by the Russians at Stalingrad. Seven Soviet armies attacked and 1.2 million shells were fired in the opening bombardment. On 30 April 1945, Hitler committed suicide rather than fall into Russian hands, but fighting in the city went on until 2 May. Typical of the propaganda of the day, the taking of the Reichstag was restaged in daylight for the cameras. There was widespread looting and the murders of German soldiers and civilians continued for weeks.

Tutorial

Progress questions
1. Why did Lenin and Trotsky misinterpret the situation in Europe in 1918–1919?
2. To what extent was Stalin's foreign policy of 1928–39 consistent?
3. Why did the Soviet Union survive the Nazi onslaught of 1941–45?

Seminar discussion
A.J.P. Taylor argued, in 1961, that Stalin had not been following a plan in his foreign policy and nor was he some leviathan (all-powerful giant) able to create a policy of his choice. Taylor suggested that Stalin was reacting to events. In the Cold War, the image of Stalin as a totalitarian dictator had perhaps obscured the way that Stalin had been forced to adapt his foreign policy. Was this the best explanation?

Practical assignment
Write a short essay (45 minutes) under timed conditions, after some preparatory notes have been made, to answer the question: 'Why were atrocities committed so frequently and so readily by the Soviet forces in the Second World War?'

Study tips
1. Communist foreign policy before the Second World War reminds us that

whilst individuals are important in shaping history, they themselves are subject to the forces acting on them and around them. Neither Lenin nor Stalin made their policy freely, and they were forced to react to events.

2. Notice how the purges, the Great Terror and Soviet Economic Policy all had an effect on the Soviet Union's fortunes in the Second World War. It is worth reviewing these sections in a summary to make sure you can account for their relative influence.

3. Stalin's actions in the Second World War, and in the Cold War to follow, reveal a great deal about Stalin's priorities. Very high on his agenda was 'security' and it could be argued that his personal security, maintaining his position of power, was the most important of all.

13

Stalinism and the Cold War

One-minute summary – After the war, Stalin was determined to seize whatever resources he could from the occupied territories and to improve security both internally and externally. He exercised all the brutality that had characterised his government in the pre-war period and he risked confrontation with the West. It was he, and the communist ideology, that were largely to blame for the development of a Cold War between East and West. It was under Stalin that the Soviet Union acquired its own atomic weapons, but the boasting of the communist regime, claiming certain inventions had been discovered in Russia long before the West and its nuclear programme, were evidence of its insecurity. Fear and suspicion pervaded every part of the Soviet Union, and these anxieties emanated from the very top. Yet when Stalin died, the fundamental apparatus of the Lenin and Stalin years was not dismantled. The Cold War continued and the Soviet Union fossilised into inefficiency, abuses of power and propaganda.

In this chapter you will learn:

▶ the genesis of the Cold War
▶ the Soviet policy in Eastern Europe
▶ Stalin's final years.

The genesis of the Cold War

The Soviet Union was devastated but Stalinism was still prevalent

The western provinces of the Soviet Union had been ravaged by the German armies and devastated by war. Millions of people had been displaced or killed. The estimated total of war dead for the Soviet Union is twenty million. One in five Belorussians had been killed or had served in a slave labour camp. Millions more, evacuated during the retreat in 1941, were not permitted to return to their homes in 1945. The survivors of the fighting who had managed to stay in their homelands had been reduced to living in caves, in pits in the ground or in wreckage. The whole country lived on starvation rations: cabbage, potatoes and beets being the staple diet. To defeat the black market, all large denomination rouble notes were declared illegal, wiping out the savings of many millions overnight. The same old work routines remained too. Ten to twelve hours a day, six days a week was the average, but the *gulag* workers worked every day. There were thousands of new arrivals in the camps. The NKVD arrested the survivors of Nazi camps, accusing them of collaboration with the enemy. They exchanged one prison camp for another. When the Allies returned Ukrainians and Cossacks who had fought on the German side to Russia, at Stalin's request, the NKVD simply shot them on the quayside.

Stalin brought in even stricter measures

Newspapers were censored twice, at the draft stage and before printing, to ensure no dissent leaked through. Stalin's wartime leadership was exaggerated still further and the Marshals, including Zhukov, were gradually downplayed. By 1948, *Pravda* did not mention the famous general at all. In another bitter twist, the Leningrad branch of the party, despite assisting in the defence of the city during the war, was purged. Andrei Zhdanov had been the party leader and he denounced his colleagues. When he died suddenly in 1948, Beria, Stalin's head of secret police, executed or exiled the rest. Even the 'Defence of Leningrad' museum was closed. Its curator was arrested.

The division of Berlin and Germany reflected growing tension between East and West

The wartime conferences between Stalin and the Western leaders, Churchill and Roosevelt, had stated that their priority was the defeat of Germany, and then supervision over spheres of influence. Churchill was conscious that Stalin had designs on Eastern Europe and he did not trust him. Relations on the river Elbe, where the Western armies met the Soviets, had initially been cordial, but it was not long before confrontation developed there too. As soon as the war ended, the Soviets had been eager to strip the occupied countries, especially Germany, of any resources. Machinery, property, but above all, men with military or scientific expertise, were taken to Russia. In one night, 22 October 1946, 6,000 scientists and military experts were seized by the Soviet Union. The famous Zeiss optical factory was moved to Moscow. The Opel car works were also taken and the Russian 'Moskovich' was a direct copy of the German car. In the Western sectors, the Americans were pumping millions of dollars under the Marshall Plan so as to get Europe back on its feet as a trading partner. The Stalinist policy was simply one of pillage. Consequently, the temporary occupation boundaries of Germany became more permanent. In 1946, Churchill warned that 'an iron curtain' had fallen across the continent. However, Berlin was in a curious situation as the Western-held sectors were in an island of communist territory.

Ideological differences were the primary cause of the Cold War

Once Germany, the common enemy, had been defeated in 1945, there was little in common between the Soviet Union and the West. The Western countries were democracies where each individual could vote according to their individual preferences without fear of intimidation. They could assemble freely, to demonstrate if they wished, or simply to voice their own opinion freely. The newspapers and radio stations were not censored, nor did they have to report any 'party line'. The Western powers were also capitalist, enabling anyone to use their own enterprise and initiative to enrich himself or herself. The focus was on supporting a consumer society, which, in turn, gave the citizens of the West material improvements. In the Eastern Bloc, there were no freedoms. One could only vote for the approved Communist Party candidate. People dare not speak their mind, lest they ended up in a police cell or a *gulag*. All media was strictly censored and controlled. There was no free enterprise, and the command economy was doomed to stagnation for another four decades. However, Stalin also shares some responsibility for the Cold War. He was determined to create satellite states in Eastern Europe, and maintained the Red Army on its wartime footing (whereas the Western Allies reduced their forces when the war was over). Harry Truman, the American president, was exasperated by the posturing of the Soviet leader: 'Only one language do they understand – "How many divisions have you?"'.

The Soviet policy in Eastern Europe

The crushing of Czech democracy in 1948 alarmed the West

The Soviet Union had ensured that puppet communist governments were installed in all its territories, namely Bulgaria, Rumania, Poland and East Germany. In Czechoslovakia, which had been a democracy before the Second World War, the NKVD intimidated, murdered, deported, banned, and rigged elections to get the results it wanted. Some leading democrats had apparently committed 'suicide'. On 10 March 1948, Jan Masaryk, the Foreign Minister, was found dead beneath a window of his apartment. A doorman had seen suspicious men enter but the official inquest recorded 'suicide' brought on by 'depression increased by Western recriminations'. The President, Benes, resigned in protest, and the Communist Party took over.

The Berlin blockade worsened relations with the West

In June 1948, Stalin ordered road and rail links between western Germany and Berlin to be cut, effectively blockading the city. He anticipated a humiliating climb down for the British, French and Americans and he believed they would not dare take on the Red Army. However, without escalating the situation, British and American aircrews began a round-the-clock airlift to Berlin, supplying it with coal and foodstuffs. Stalin may have thought that, as in the dying days of the German garrison at Stalingrad, his enemies would not be able to keep up the supplies, but they did and Stalin was forced to call off his blockade in May 1949. The Americans had been quite prepared to take on the Red Army too, and at this stage they were the only power with an atomic bomb. Once again, Stalin's foreign policy had failed.

Stalinist policy in the East was as ruthless as ever

Stalin continued to root out his opponents, both real and imagined, inside the vast territory he now controlled. The Baltic states were one of the first post-war targets, where 400,000 Estonians, Lithuanians and Latvians were deported to Siberia to join lumber camps and mines. Many other nationalities suffered the same fate, being forced to work relentlessly in sub-zero temperatures. At the uranium mines at Butuguchak in Siberia, the inmates died of radiation sickness in three months. Cramped in barrack blocks, those that worked in the ore processing plant survived only thirty shifts. At Vorkuta, former army officers who had been sentenced for criticism of Stalin, despite suffering the hardships of the war, revolted in 1948 and killed their guards. They were massacred. Another revolt at a Vorkuta women's camp in 1953 was crushed by tanks driving over the prisoners, whilst squads of machine gunners roamed the huts, shooting anyone inside.

The first Soviet atomic bomb was detonated in 1949

Thanks to Soviet spies and conscripted scientists, the Russians successfully detonated their first atomic bomb on 29 August 1949. It was a significant moment historically, for the Soviet Union had one of the world's largest armies and it was able to confront the West militarily. The response in the West was to close ranks and create the North Atlantic Treaty Organisation (NATO). The terms stated clearly that an attack on any member would be construed as an attack on them all. Collective security had been achieved but it was aimed at the Soviet Union. Stalin's reaction was to embark on a nuclear weapon-building programme regardless of cost. His obsession with security kept the Soviet Union, and its economy, on a permanent war footing. In the long term this was to prove damaging.

Stalin's final years

Stalinist Russia seemed to lose touch with reality in the final years of the dictator's life. The Russians began to claim that they had invented the incandescent lamp before Edison, they had invented the Morse code before Samuel Morse, radio before Marconi and even penicillin before Fleming. The Soviets also claimed they had been the first to invent powered flight. Newspapers reported most of their news about Stalin, and radio broadcasts mentioned his name in practically every sentence. His image was everywhere, in paintings, photographs, busts, and statues.

Stalin's death was a gruesome end to a brutal life

Stalin's paranoia began to affect everyone. Making a huge espionage effort themselves, the Soviets feared spies everywhere. His insecurity was such that if he travelled by train, every station along the route was cleared. If he moved by car, the roads were deserted. He confined himself to a *dacha* outside Moscow, where the doors were protected by thick steel. Fearing poison, he would eat nothing until it had been tasted. Food was delivered through a hatch. As he grew older, he accused his doctor, Yakob Rapaport, of conspiring against him and all doctors were condemned as belonging to a Jewish plot. Soviet citizens stopped attending doctors' surgeries and hundreds were imprisoned. An anti-Semitic mania began to sweep the country. On 1 March 1953, Stalin suffered a brain haemorrhage and fell into a coma. In the final moments, with twisted features and blackened lips, he revived. His daughter recorded: 'he cast a terrible glance, insane or perhaps angry and full of fear of death'. Raising his arm as if to accuse, or perhaps curse, he collapsed – dead.

Conclusions

Across the *gulags*, there were riots and celebrations at the news of Stalin's death. Beria, Stalin's chief henchman, was swiftly tried and executed, gagged so that he could not give away the names of his fellow murderers who presided over his death. However, the *gulags* did not completely disappear, and the apparatus of Party dictatorship survived. Fear and suspicion remained endemic in the Soviet Union. The statues of Stalin did not last, but the propaganda and the 'double speak' did. Hungarians in 1956 and the Czechs in 1968 felt the full force of the Soviet fist when they tried to express their independence. The Red Army continued to be maintained at a strength far exceeding the West, and the nuclear weapons programme begun in 1949 escalated into an arms race with the United States. The Soviet Union's Interior Ministry also had thousands of troops to crush any internal opposition within the Soviet Union. The attempts to cover up the mistakes that surrounded the Chernobyl nuclear accident in 1986 typified the old communist lies. Nevertheless, the Cold War ensured that this brand of communism was contained until it collapsed under the weight of its own inefficiency in 1991. There was a genuine feeling of liberation across Eastern Europe and in the former Soviet Union when the old regimes passed away, and despite efforts by communists to rebrand themselves as socialist or democratic, their ideology had been discredited.

Tutorial

Progress questions
1. What were Stalin's priorities in 1945–49?
2. Why did a Cold War develop between East and West in 1945–49?
3. Why did so little change within the Soviet Union after the Second World War?

Seminar discussion
How far was Stalin responsible for the development of the Cold War?

Practical assignment
Consider reviewing this book by skimming through the headings. This will help you to commit the main themes to memory and is an effective way to revise.

Glossary

Agitprop Agitation propaganda – a campaign launched soon after the revolution to persuade the people of Russia to support the Bolsheviks.

Autocracy Rule by one leader with extensive powers. A dictatorship without necessarily having full control of the population (see **Totalitarianism**).

Bolshevism Name given to communism in the early twentieth century.

Capitalism An economic system that favours free and unlimited business. By allowing free enterprise, capitalism ensures that the innovative and entrepreneurial spirit of a population is able to maximise the exploitation of resources to generate wealth.

Cheka The Soviet secret police, 1917–22.

Chiski Cleansings – purges of the Communist Party.

Collectivisation The pooling of agricultural resources in state run units as opposed to the free enterprise of independent farmers. Collectivisation involved the conscription of rural people.

Comintern Communist International.

Commissar Political agent or delegate of communism.

Communism The political and economic philosophy of states that aspire to total equality in society, even if that equality has to be enforced. Communists believe that power must be acquired by revolution, and that a period of dictatorship by the people (or a party) is essential to destroy and dismantle capitalism.

Duma A Russian parliament or Constituent Assembly.

Fascism The rule of a dictator whilst mobilising mass support and espousing the benefits of extreme nationalism and action. Historically confined to Italy between 1922 and 1943, the term became a common yardstick for the right-wing movements of Europe in the 1930s and 1940s.

Glasnost 'Openness' – the idea that all aspects of Soviet society should be open to inspection and that there should be honesty about problems, rather than the veneer of propaganda which had always concealed the truth.

Gosplan The planning committee that ran five year plans.

Gulag Forced labour camp.

Internationalism The idea that international considerations should take precedence over national, regional or local ones. Internationalists of the 1920–40s were left-wingers who believed that the solution to social, economic and political problems lay in international co-operation, led by the Soviet Union.

Kadets Constitutional Democratic Party.

KGB The Soviet Secret Service from the 1950s.

Kolkhoz Collective farm communities run by the state.

Kulaks Derogatory term to describe richer farmers.

Leninism The brand of communism associated with Lenin, namely a revolutionary elite that initiates, directs and sustains revolutionary action and which governs in the name of the people.

Mir Village commune.

MRC Military Revolutionary Committee – the body that planned the October 1917 *coup d'etat*.

Nationalisation State ownership of the economy; the opposite of capitalism.

NEP New Economic Policy – The Soviet name for reintroducing capitalism temporarily in the Russian economy in 1921.

NKVD Soviet secret police, 1934–43.

Nomenklatura A list of loyal personnel drawn up in the 1920s to exclude the 'fellow travellers who had joined the Communist Party allegedly for reasons of opportunism'. The Nomenklatura became a new elite in Russia to replace the old aristocracy and bourgeoisie and it marked the beginning of Party membership as the passport of elitism.

Ochrana Secret police.

OGPU The Soviet secret police, 1922–34.

perestoika Reform of economic and political systems.

pogroms Anti-Semitic riots.

Politburo Controlling committee of the Communist Party, consisting of 7–9 members.

Pravda 'Truth' – the name of the official state newspaper.

Proletariat Urban working class.

Rabkhrin Workers and Peasants Inspectorate.

Red Army The title of the army of the Soviet Union, hence 'Reds' were all Communists.

Rightists Term used to describe opponents of Stalin who exhibited a 'right (wing) deviation' even though this accusation was untrue.

Socialism Philosophy that advocates egalitarianism and state ownership without necessarily using violent means or force. The term was used interchangeably with communism to persuade all those on the left to follow the lead of the communists.

Socialist Realism Art genre that showed the workers in a heroic light.

Soviets Councils.

Sovnarkom Council of People's Commissars – the Cabinet that ran the Soviet Union after the Revolution until 1941. Each member (of which there were 30) ran a commissariat or department. After 1919 it was largely superseded by the smaller *Politiburo*.

Stakhanovites Workers who emulated the labours of Alexei Stakhanov to exceed targets for productivity.

Totalitarianism The concept of total control of society by means of political institutions, secret police, informers and public rituals.

Ukase Edicts.

War Communism Requisition of food to feed the army and the cities.

Zemstva Regional councils in Tsarist Russia.

Useful Websites

General Russian history
http://www.slavweb.com/eng/Russia/history-e.html This site covers all periods and issues with documents and articles.

The Tsarist regime
http://www.alexanderpalace.org/palace/mainpage.html Details of the Tsars, their families and their fate, details of the palaces and a virtual tour of the Winter Palace.
http://www2.sptimes.com/Treasures/tc.2.3.19.html Nicholas II's brief biography from the St Petersburg Times of Russia.

The Russian Imperial Navy
http://webpdp.gator/v3/webpdp_v3_plugin.php?yic = HIC_fortunecityDT4

Sergei Witte and industrialisation
www.dur.ac.uk/~dml0www/witte.html Witte's own words on 'tasks for economic policy'.
http://members.tripod.com~american_almanac/witte92a.htm With 92b.htm, two sources on Witte's policy.

Abdication
www.pp.clinet.fi/~pkr01/history/abdic.html Notes and documents on the Tsar's final months as ruler of Russia.

Lenin
www.Marxists.org/archive/Lenin/index.htm Lenin's works, words, and images.
www.marx2mao.org/Lenin/index.htm Original works by Lenin.
www.stel.ru/museum/Lenin_childhood.htm Lenin's life in photos with an interesting text.
www.aha.ru/~mausoleu/index A visit, including VR visit, to Lenin's tomb.
www.bbc.co.uk/education/modern/russia/russihtm Lenin, the October Revolution and Civil War with accompanying questions.

Stalin
www.marx2mao.org/Stalin.index.html A database of primary source materials on Stalin.
www.bbc.co.uk/education/modern/Stalin/stlihtm A good clear introduction to the subject, laid out in questions with bullet point answers.
http://www.osa.ceu.hu/gulag A site devoted to the Stalinist camps with a set of links.
www.stalin.narod.ru/ (For death of Stalin.) Images, quotes and appraisal.

Cold War
http://wwics.si.edu/index.cfm?fureaction = topics.home&topic_id1409 There are many site on this vast topic and an advanced search on Google would be the most profitable approach.

Selected Further Reading

The Revolutions of 1917

Abraham, Richard, *Alexander Kerensky: The First Love of the Revolution* (New York, 1987). An important study of a person rarely treated.

Acton, Edward, *Rethinking the Russian Revolution* (London, 1990). An analysis of the historiography before the recent opening of the Soviet Archives.

Figes, Orlando, *A People's Tragedy: The Russian Revolution, 1891–1924* (London, 1997). A critical view of the revolution and its effects.

Pipes, Richard, *Three Whys of the Russian Revolution* (London, 1998) An up-to-date assessment of the revolution which incorporates the new revisionism. See also his *Concise History of the Russian Revolution*, 1995.

Reed, John, *Ten Days that Shook the World* (1919, various reprints). As the title suggests, Reed was totally enamoured by the Russian Revolution and presented the Bolshevik seizure of power as an entirely reasonable event.

Service, Robert, *The Russian Revolution, 1900–27*, 2nd edn., (London, 1991). A leading short study.

Seton-Watson, H., *The Decline of Imperial Russia 1855–1914* (London, 1952). A classic of its time.

Williams, Beryl, *The Russian Revolution, 1917–32* (London, 1987). An excellent standard work on the revolutionary period.

Economic Policies

Davies, R.W., *Soviet Economic Development from Stalin to Krushchev* (Cambridge, 1998). An excellent study of the subject.

Mosse, W.E., *An Economic History of Russia, 1856–1914* (London, 1996). Regarded as an excellent study of the economic condition of Russia before the revolution.

Nove, Alec, *An Economic History of the USSR* (1976). Still the leading accessible study of the subject from the Tsarist period onwards.

Lenin

Laver, John, *Lenin* (London, 1993). A brief introduction.

Pipes, Richard, ed., *The Unknown Lenin: From the Soviet Archives* (USA: Yale, 1996). A critical new study making use of the archives opened after the fall of the

Soviet Union.

Service, Robert, *Lenin* (London, 2000). Also based on the archives, Service tries to present a balanced account of Lenin's life but the flaws in Vladmir Illyich are all too apparent.

Shub, David, *Lenin* (1966). A highly critical view by a contemporary.

Volkogonov, Dmitri, *Lenin's Life and Legacy* (London, 1994).

Stalin

Fitzpatrick, Sheila, *Stalinism, New Directions* (London, 2000). The revisionist view of Stalinist Russia.

Volkogonov, Dmitri, *Stalin's Triumph and Tragedy* (London, 1991).

The Terror

Conquest, Robert, *The Great Terror: A Reassessment* (London, 1990). Stalin portrayed as the prime cause of the purges and architect of the Terror.

Getty, J.A., and O.V. Naumov, *The Road to Terror: Stalin and the Self-Destruction of the Bolsheviks* (USA: Yales, 1999). The most recent of Getty's views that suggest Stalin was not the *only* reason for the Great Terror.

Ward, C., ed., *The Stalinist Dictatorship* (London, 1998).

The wider context

Hosking, G., *A History of the Soviet Union* (London, 1985). A concise introduction.

Moynahan, Brian, *The Russian Century* (1994). An attractive illustrated history.

Orwell, George, *1984* (London, 1948). Unmissable and frightening.

Sakwa, Richard, *The Rise and Fall of the Soviet Union, 1917–91* (London, 1999). An excellent source-based study.

Solzhenitsyn, A., *The Gulag Archipelago*, 2 vols. (Collins, 1974). A classic work.

Westwood, J., *Endurance and Endeavour* (Oxford, 1973). A classic.

Index